DUNGEON SIEGE ®

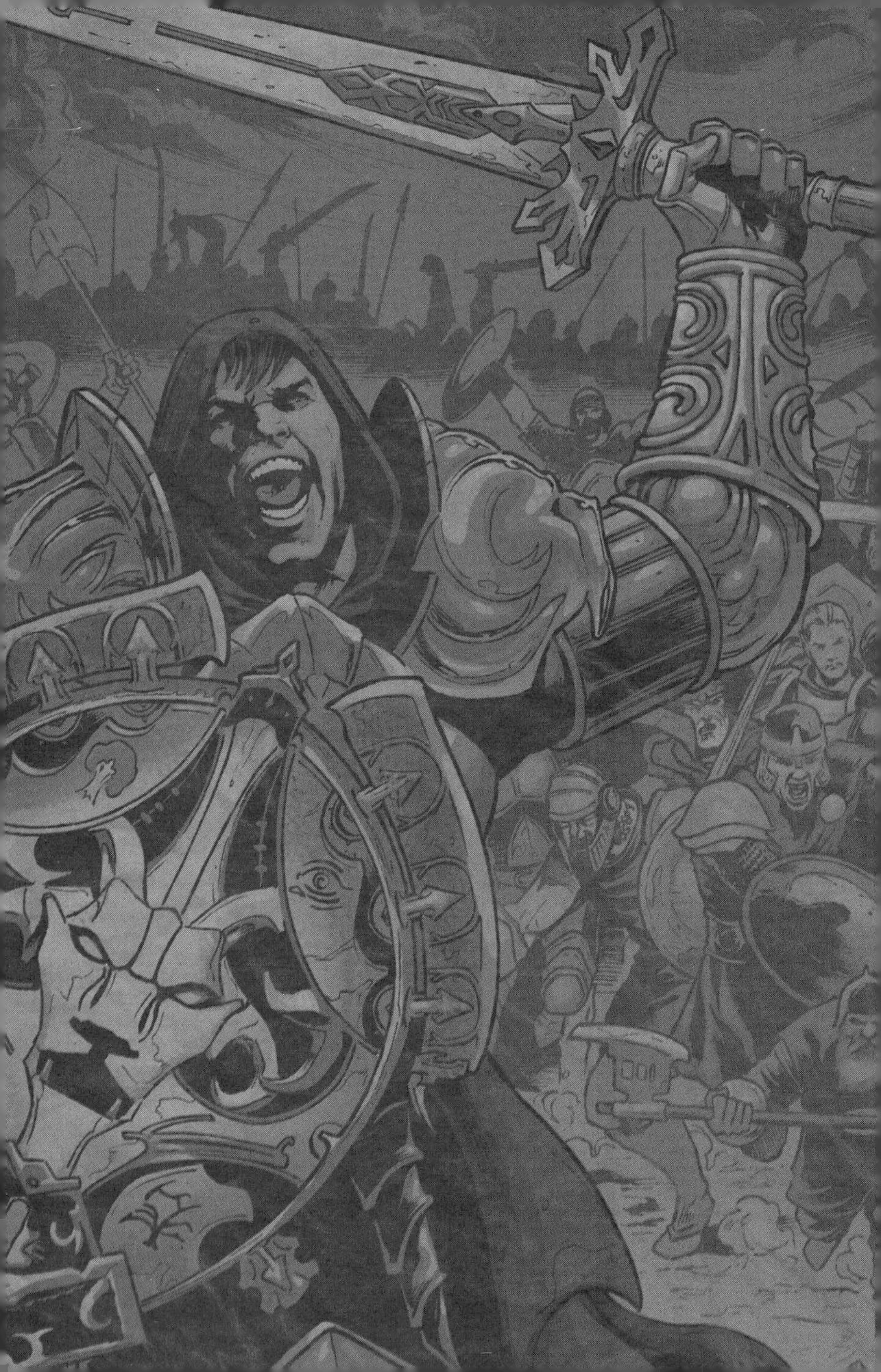

DUNGEON SIEGE®

THE BATTLE FOR ARANNA

SCRIPT
Paul Alden

LINE ART
Al Rio, Cliff Richards,
and Fabiano Neves

COLORS
Michelle Madsen, Dan Jackson,
and Michael Atiyeh

LETTERS
Michael David Thomas

COVER
r.k. post

Dark Horse Books™

Publisher » Mike Richardson

Editor » Dave Land

Assistant Editor » Katie Moody

Designer » Heidi Fainza

Special thanks to Steve Thompson, Kevin Pun,
and Jason Willig at Gas Powered Games

DUNGEON SIEGE: THE BATTLE FOR ARANNA

Dark Horse Books
A division of Dark Horse Comics, Inc.
10956 SE Main Street
Milwaukie, OR 97222

darkhorse.com

To find a comics shop in your area,
call the Comic Shop Locator Service
toll-free at (888) 266-4226

First edition: June 2005
ISBN: 1-59307-425-5

1 3 5 7 9 10 8 6 4 2
PRINTED IN CANADA

Table of Contents

Script » Paul Alden
Letters » Michael David Thomas

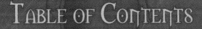

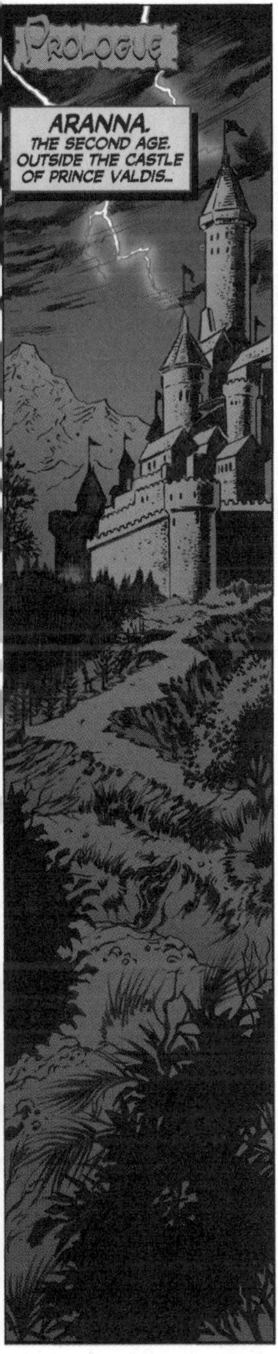
PROLOGUE
ARANNA.
THE SECOND AGE.
OUTSIDE THE CASTLE
OF PRINCE VALDIS...

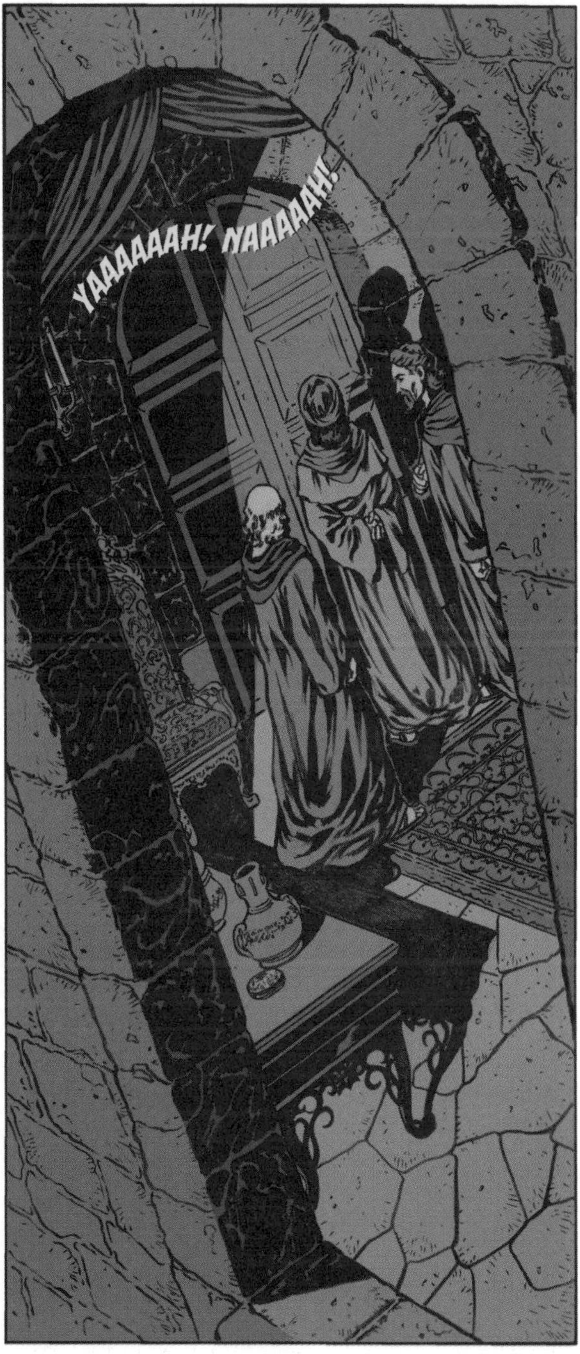
YAAAAAAH! NAAAAAH!

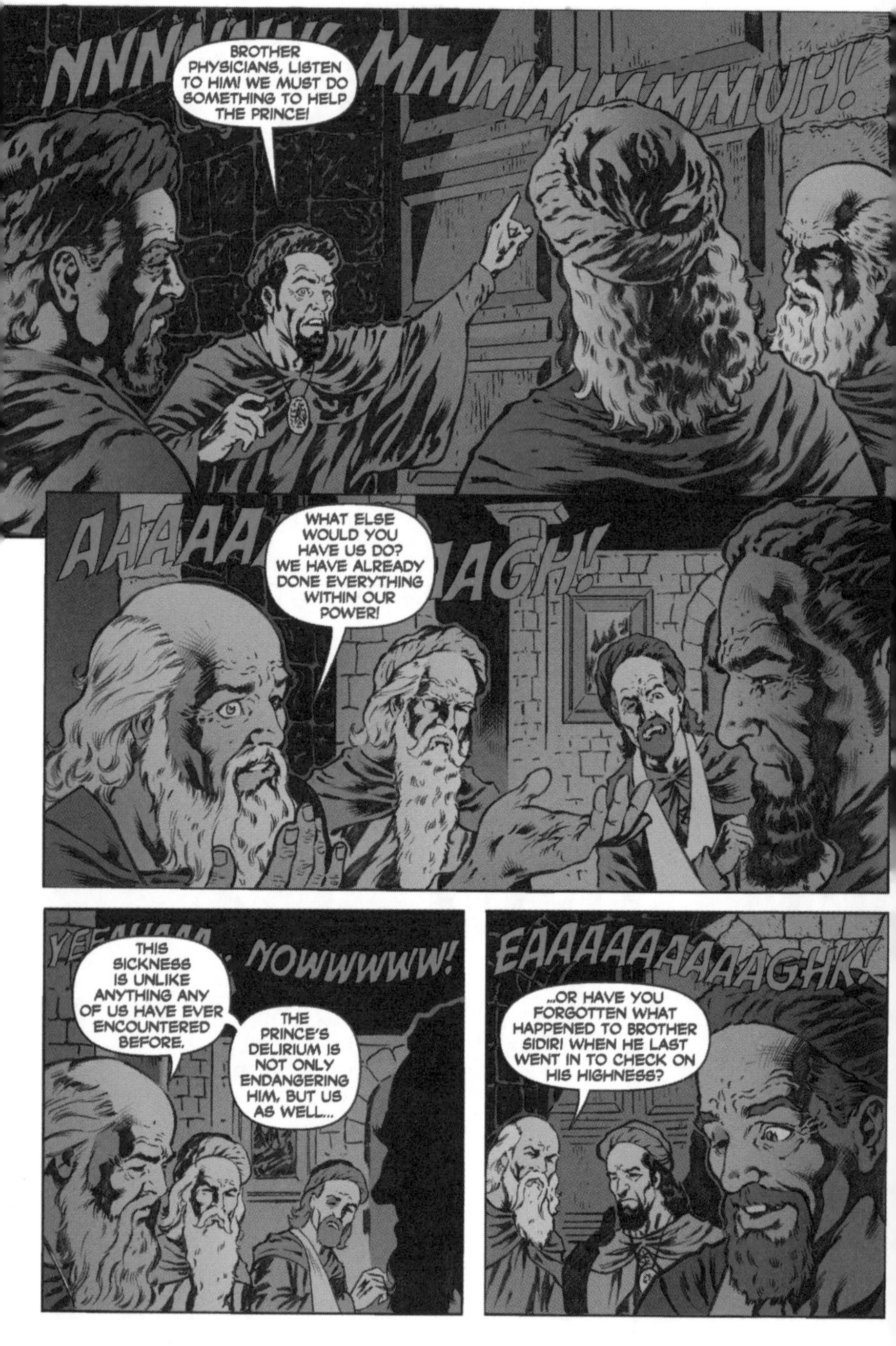
BROTHER PHYSICIANS, LISTEN TO HIM! WE MUST DO SOMETHING TO HELP THE PRINCE!
WHAT ELSE WOULD YOU HAVE US DO? WE HAVE ALREADY DONE EVERYTHING WITHIN OUR POWER!
NOWWWWWW!
THIS SICKNESS IS UNLIKE ANYTHING ANY OF US HAVE EVER ENCOUNTERED BEFORE.
THE PRINCE'S DELIRIUM IS NOT ONLY ENDANGERING HIM, BUT US AS WELL...
EAAAAAAAAAGHK!
...OR HAVE YOU FORGOTTEN WHAT HAPPENED TO BROTHER SIDIR! WHEN HE LAST WENT IN TO CHECK ON HIS HIGHNESS?

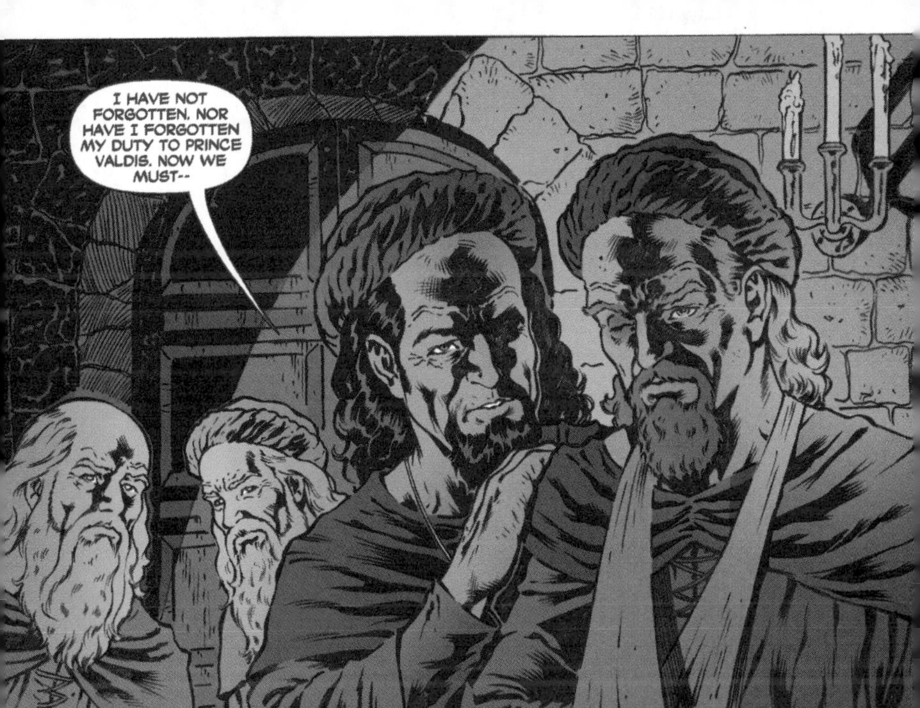
I HAVE NOT FORGOTTEN. NOR HAVE I FORGOTTEN MY DUTY TO PRINCE VALDIS. NOW WE MUST--

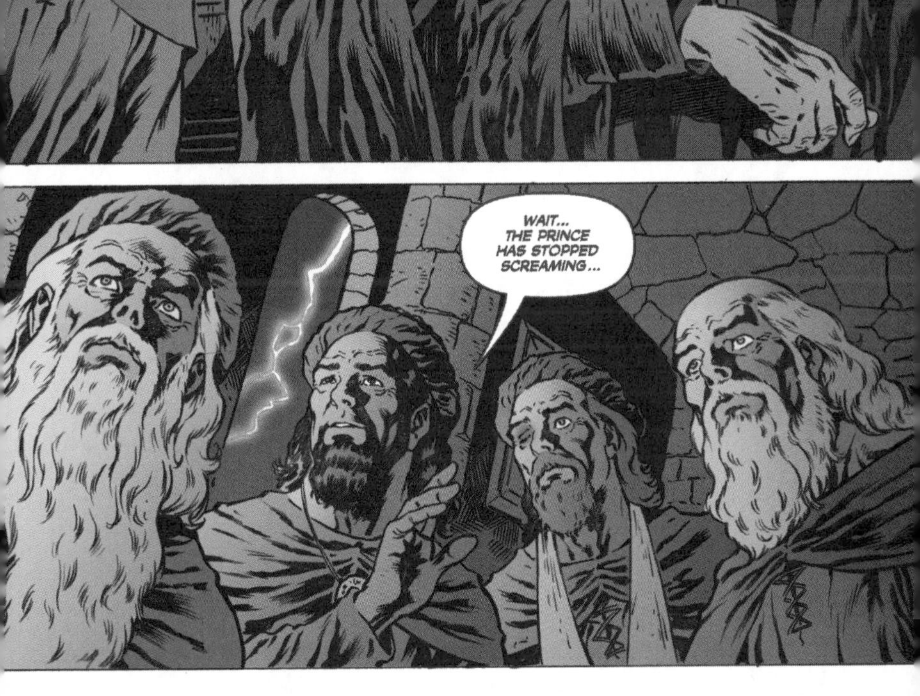
WAIT... THE PRINCE HAS STOPPED SCREAMING...

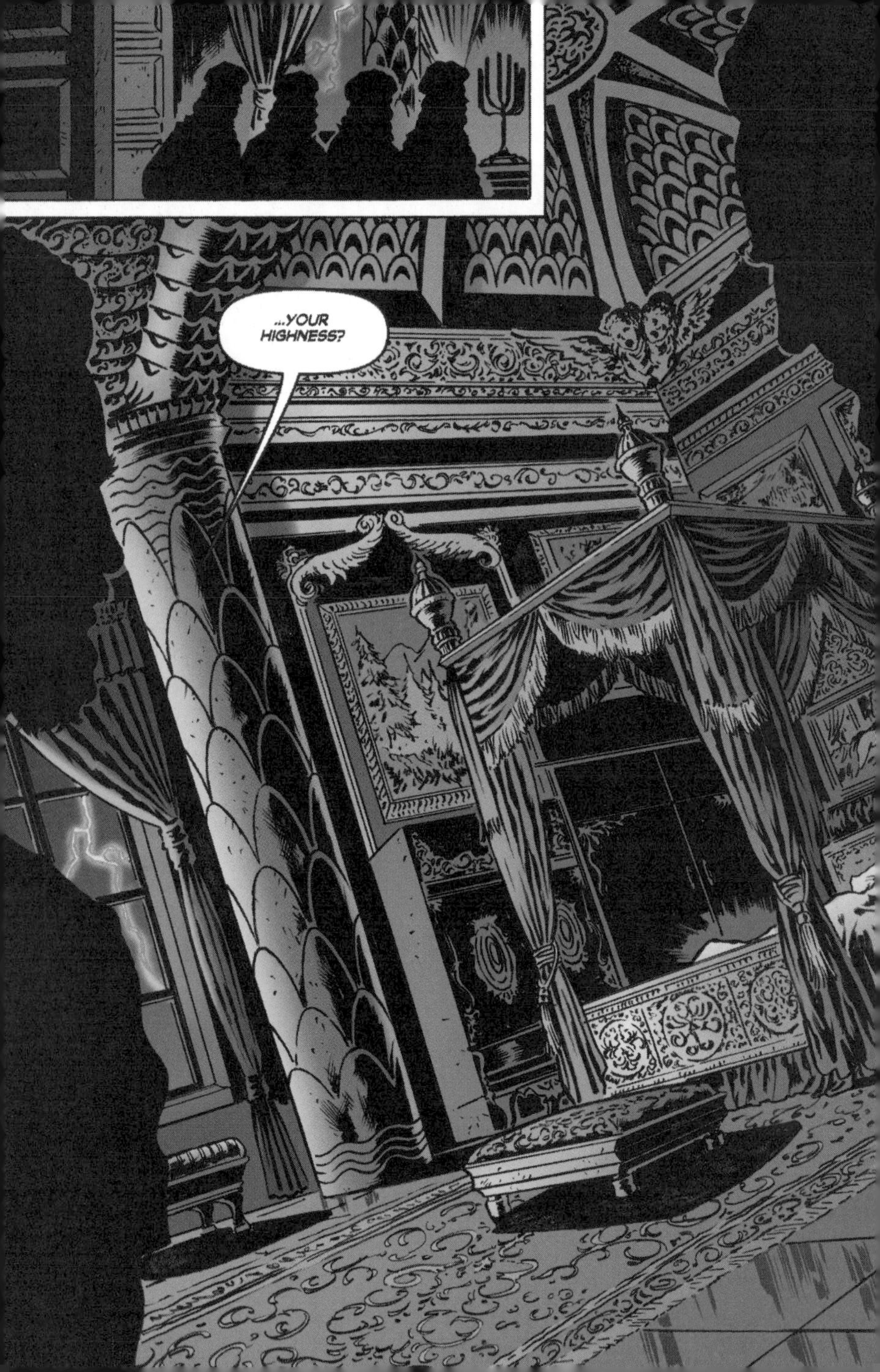
...YOUR HIGHNESS?

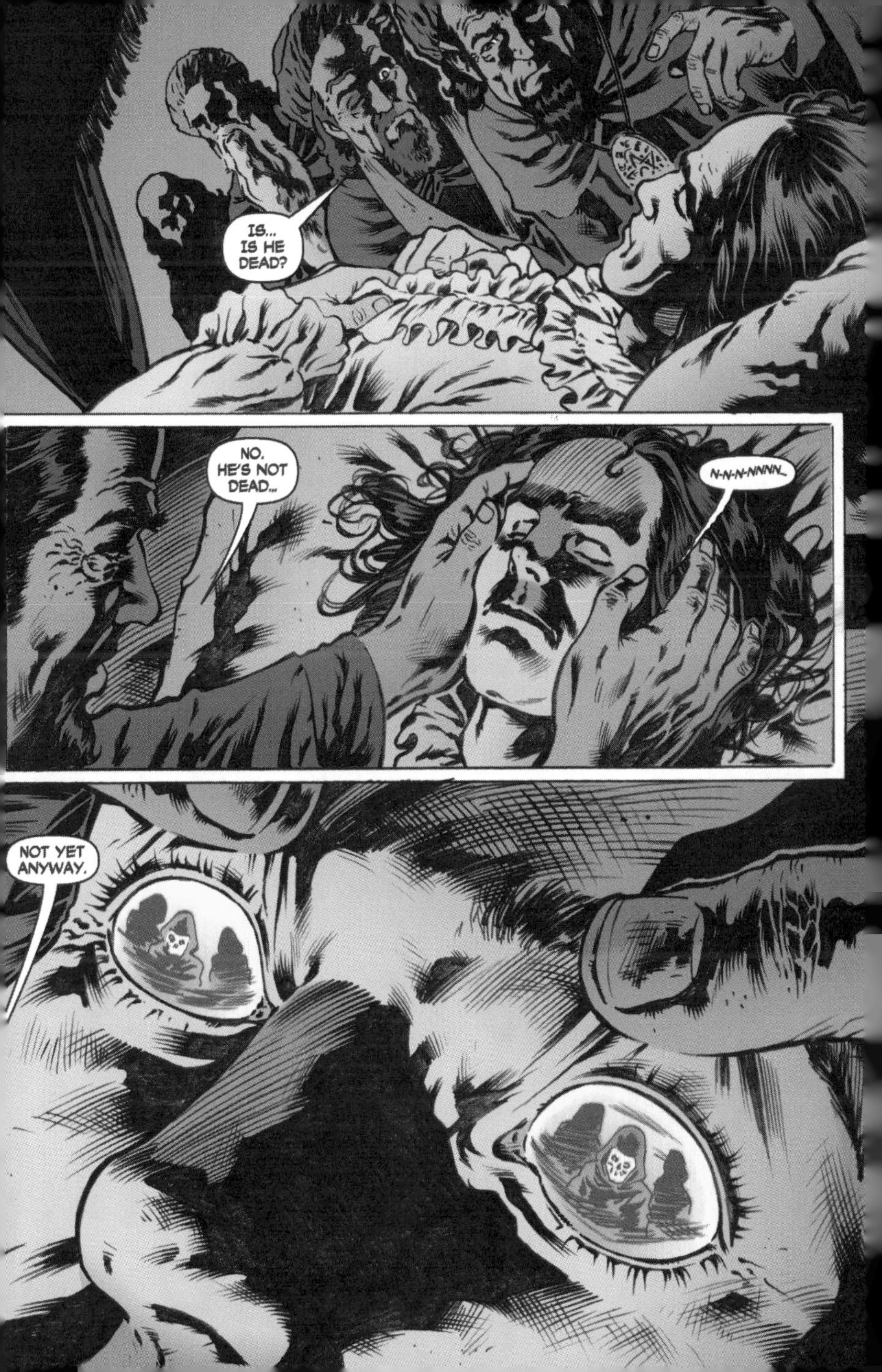
IS... IS HE DEAD?
NO. HE'S NOT DEAD...
N-N-N-NNNN...
NOT YET ANYWAY.

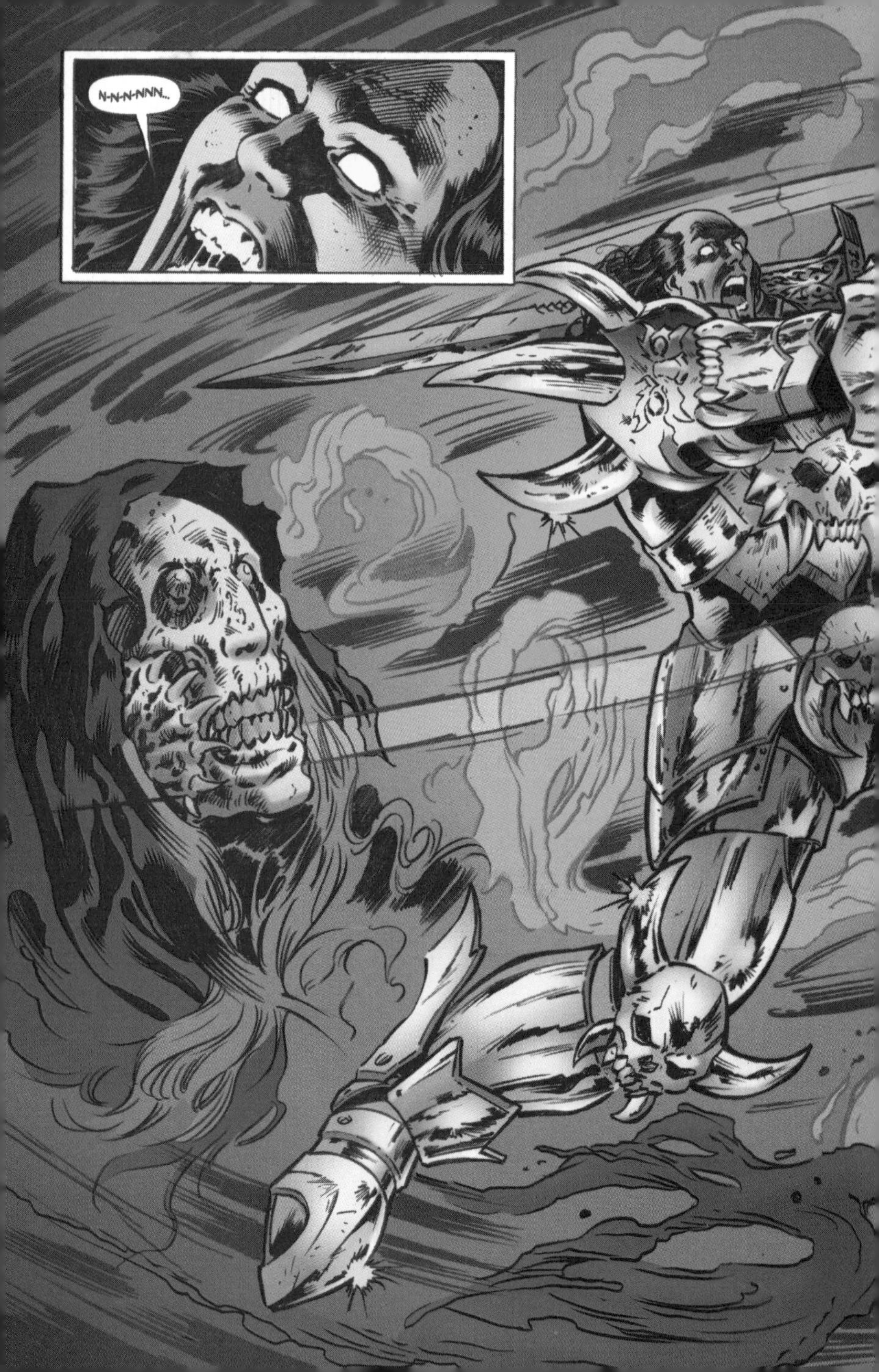
N-N-N-NNN...

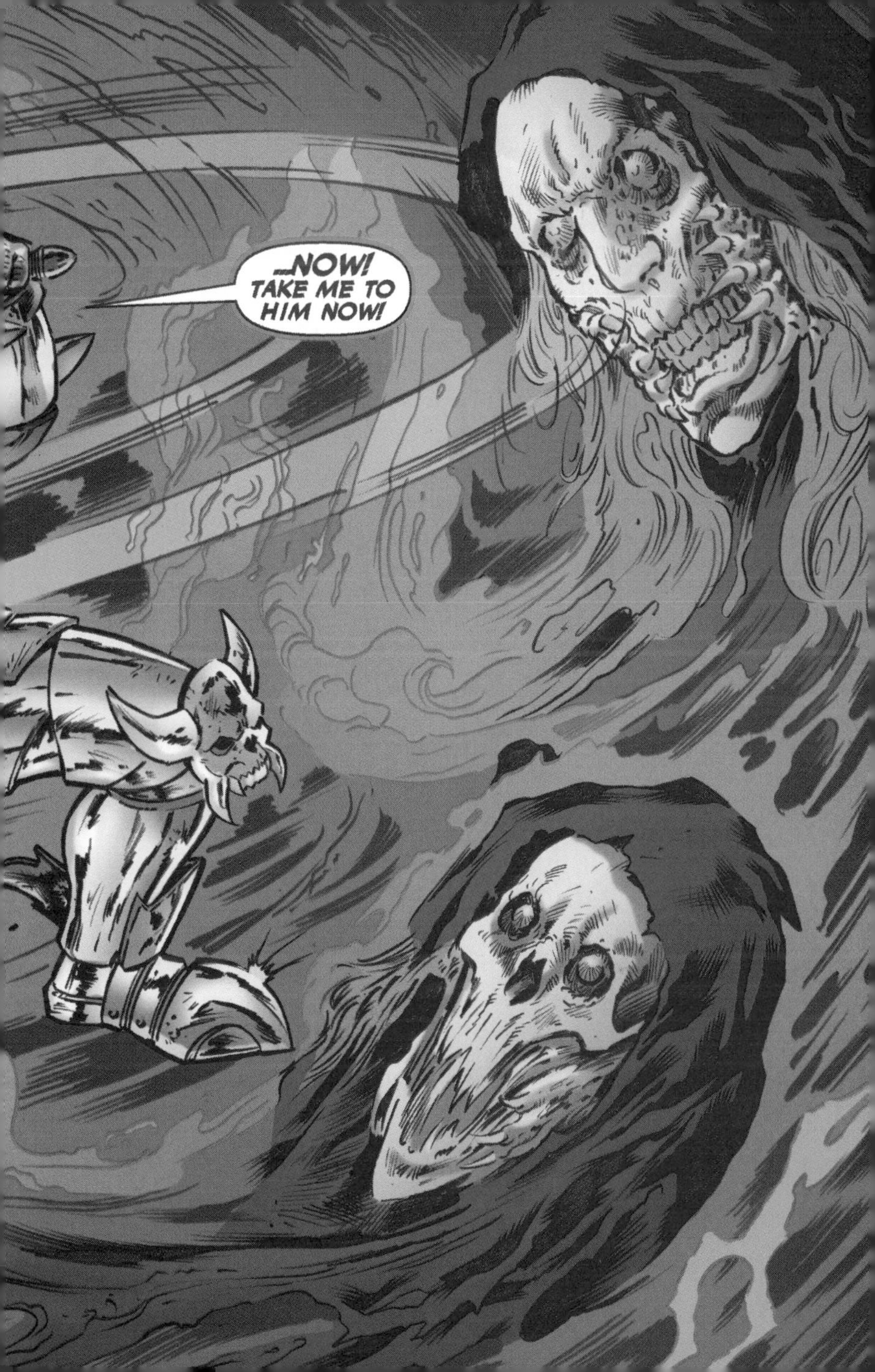
...NOW! TAKE ME TO HIM NOW!

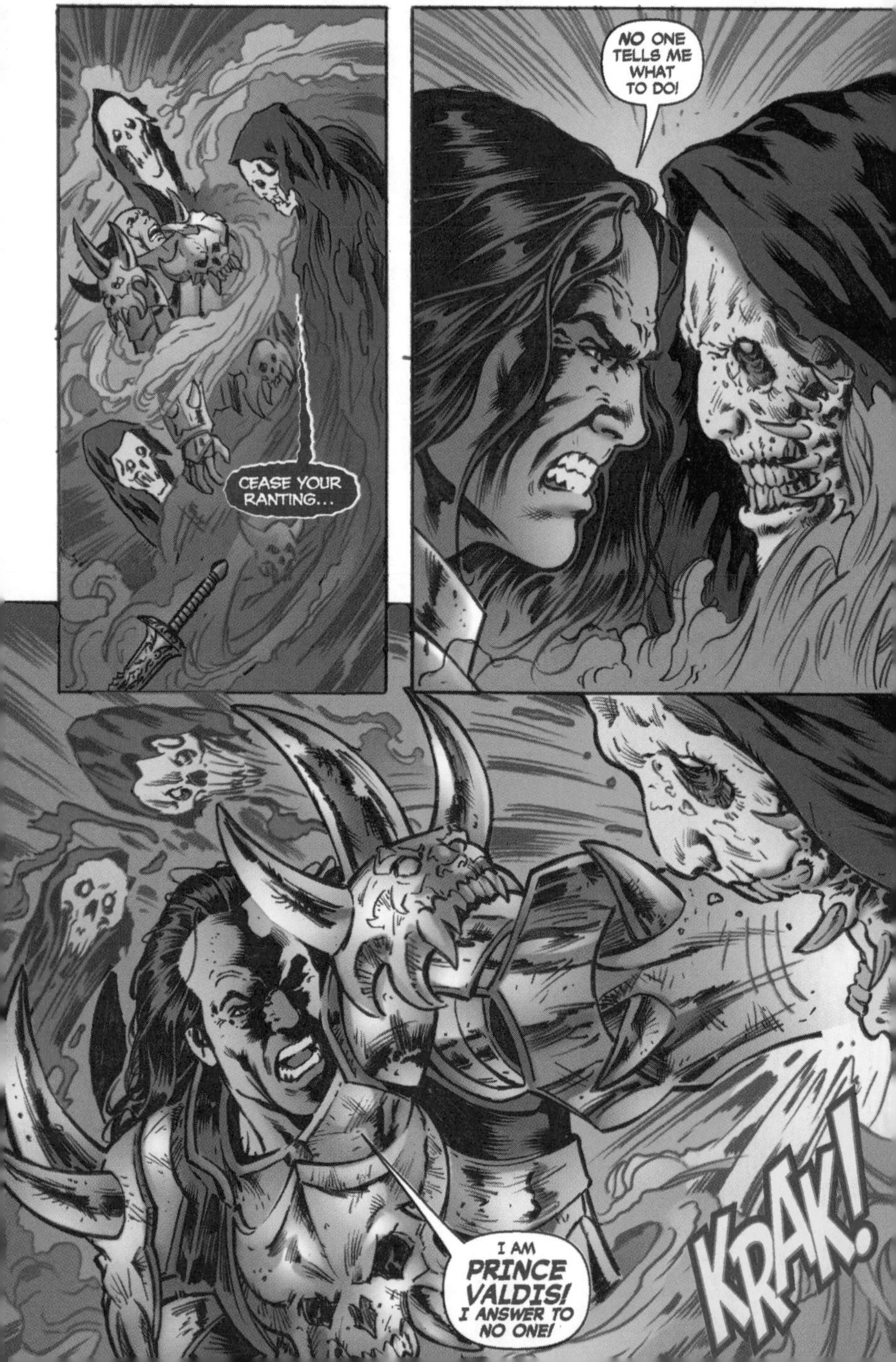
CEASE YOUR RANTING...
NO ONE TELLS ME WHAT TO DO!
I AM PRINCE VALDIS! I ANSWER TO NO ONE!
KRAK!

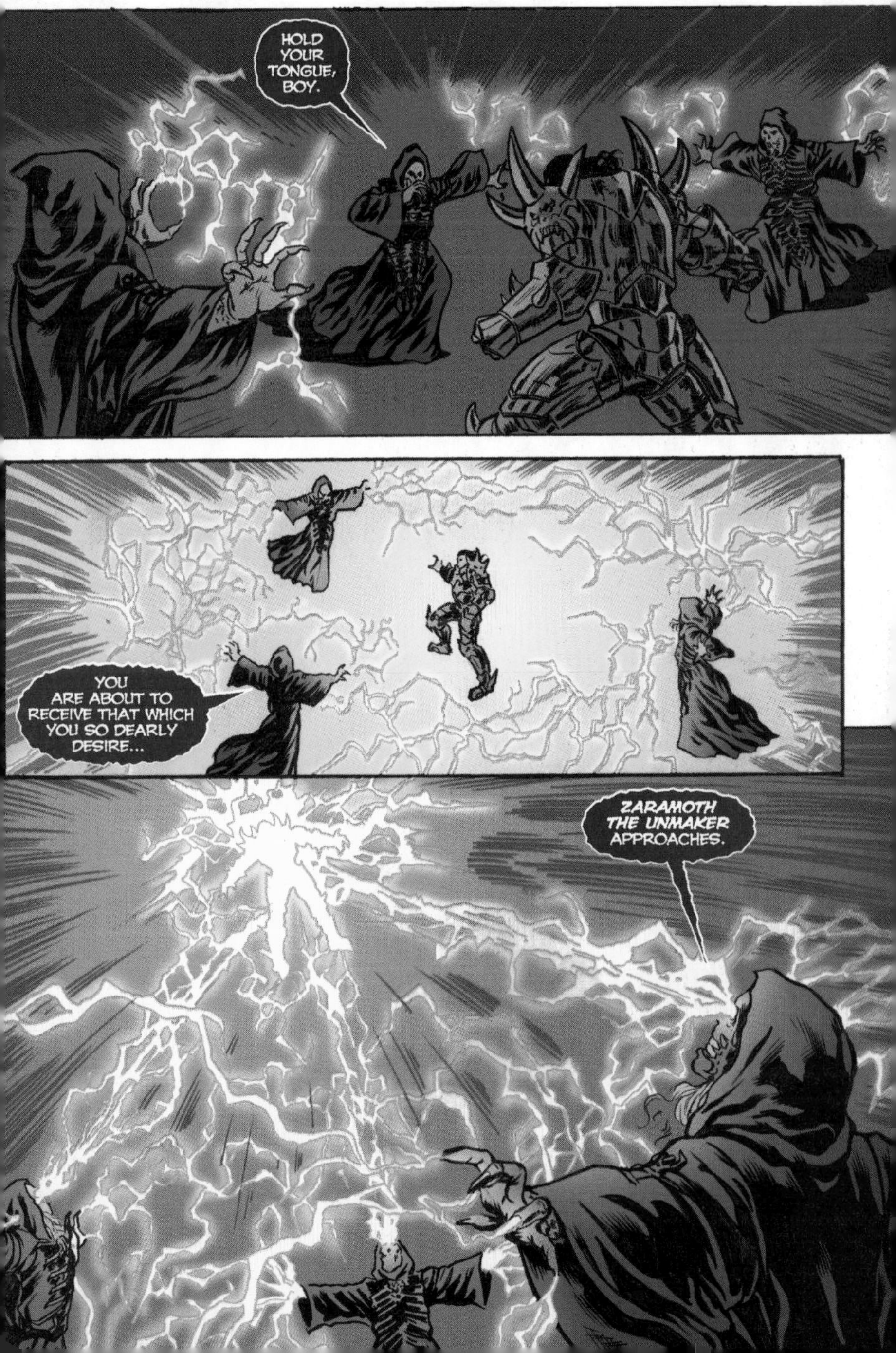
HOLD YOUR TONGUE, BOY.
YOU ARE ABOUT TO RECEIVE THAT WHICH YOU SO DEARLY DESIRE...
ZARAMOTH THE UNMAKER APPROACHES.

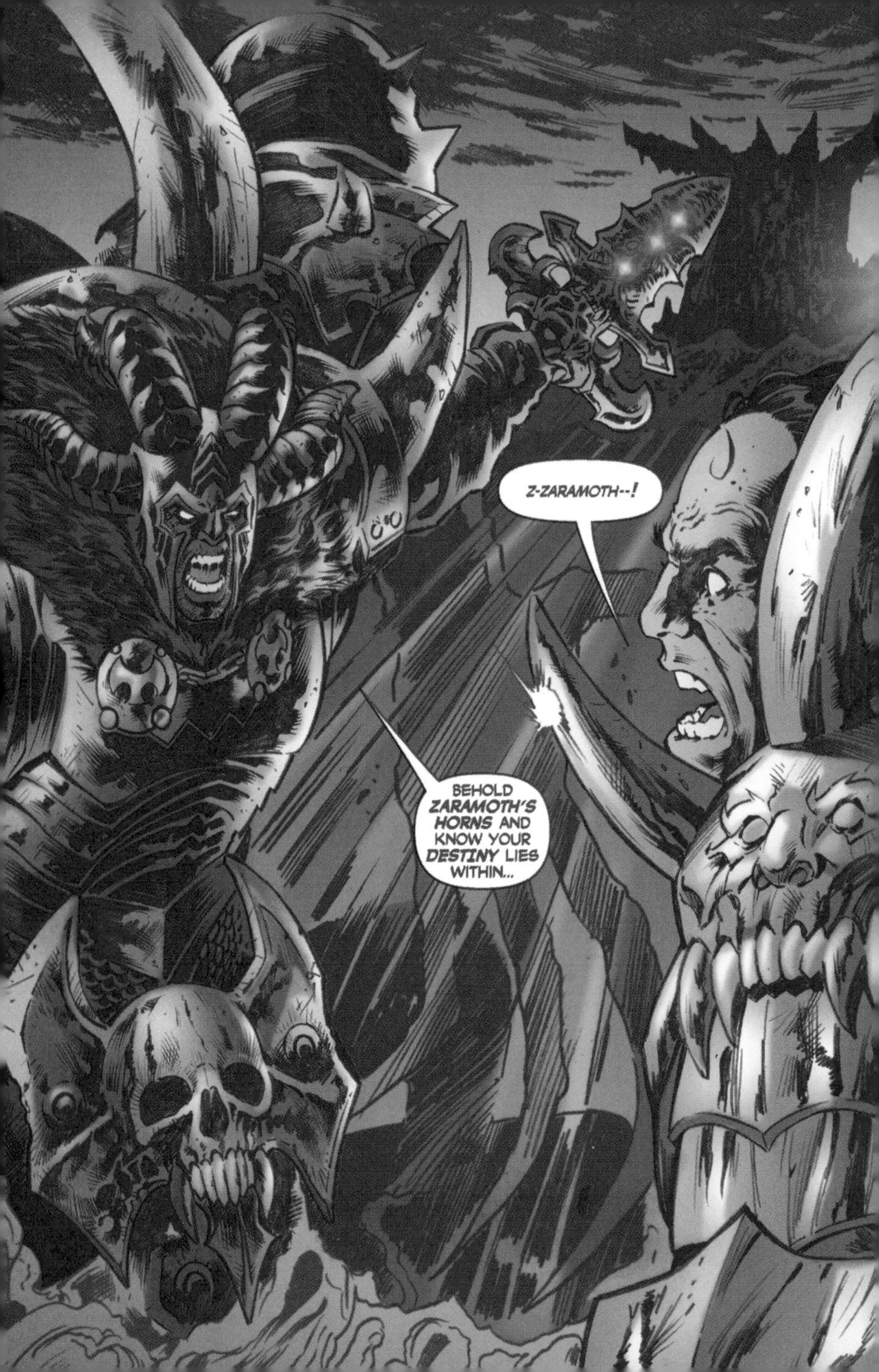
Z-ZARAMOTH--!
BEHOLD ZARAMOTH'S HORNS AND KNOW YOUR DESTINY LIES WITHIN...

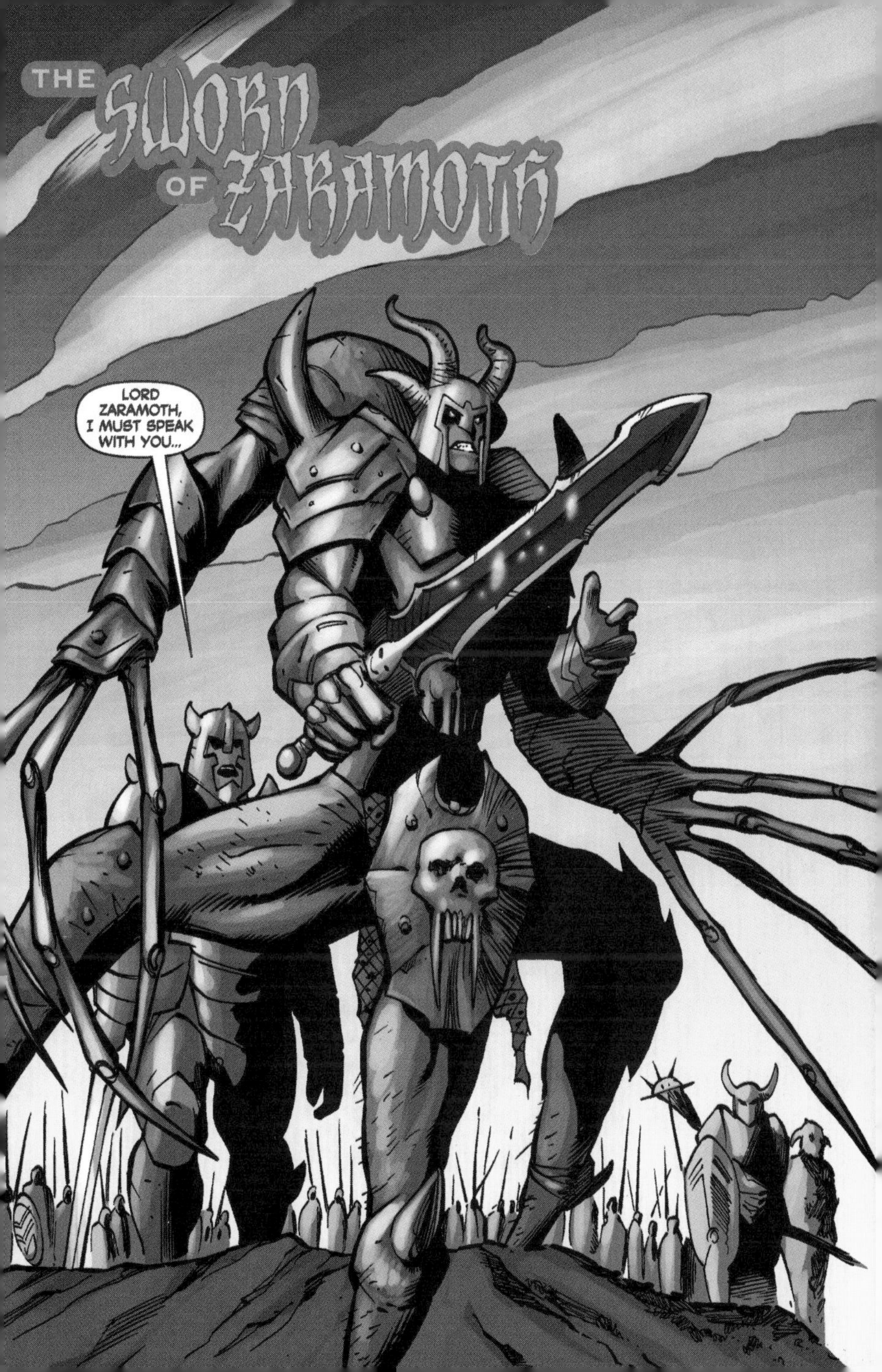
THE SWORD OF ZARAMOTH
LORD ZARAMOTH, I MUST SPEAK WITH YOU...

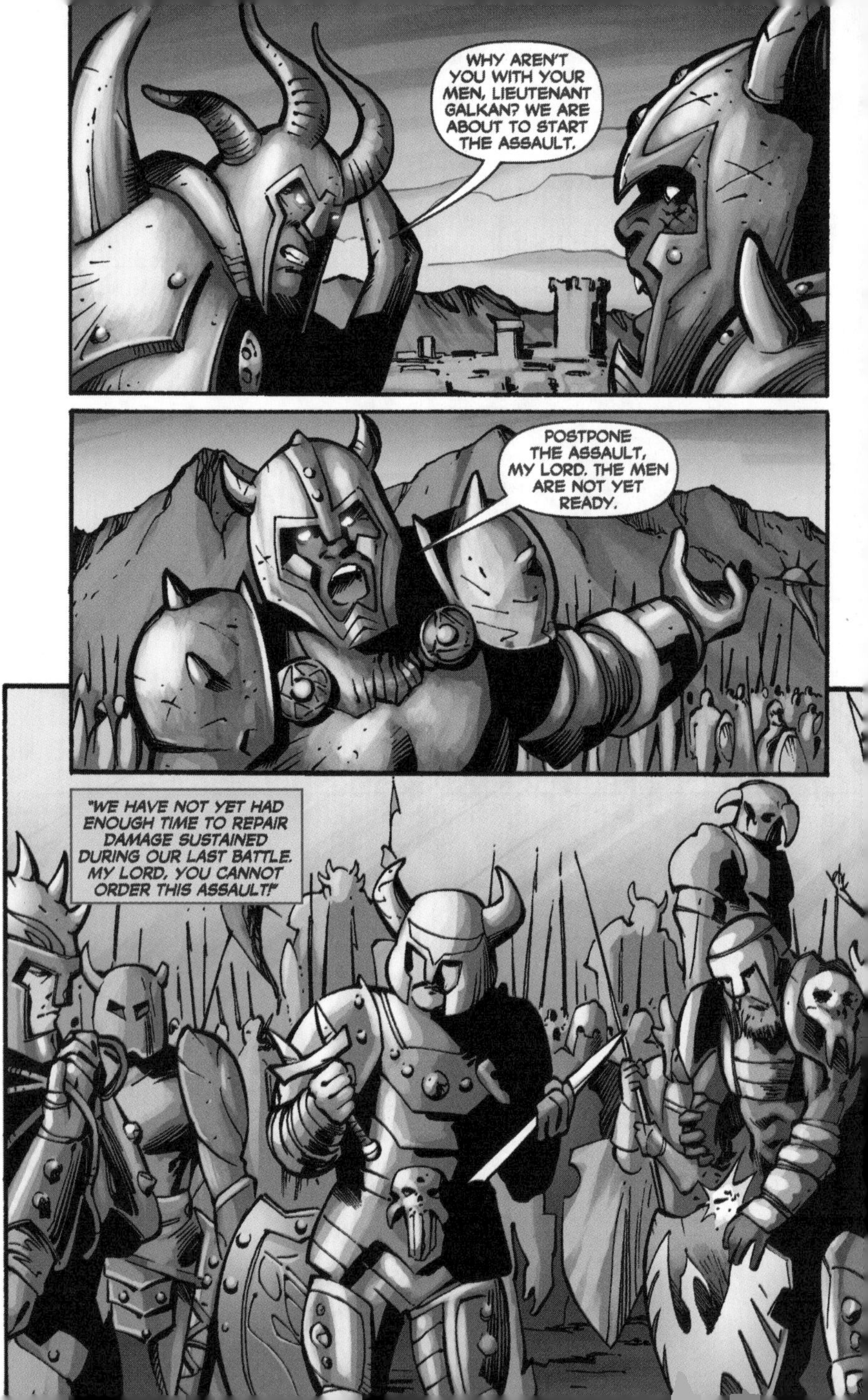
WHY AREN'T YOU WITH YOUR MEN, LIEUTENANT GALKAN? WE ARE ABOUT TO START THE ASSAULT.
POSTPONE THE ASSAULT, MY LORD. THE MEN ARE NOT YET READY.
"WE HAVE NOT YET HAD ENOUGH TIME TO REPAIR DAMAGE SUSTAINED DURING OUR LAST BATTLE. MY LORD, YOU CANNOT ORDER THIS ASSAULT!"

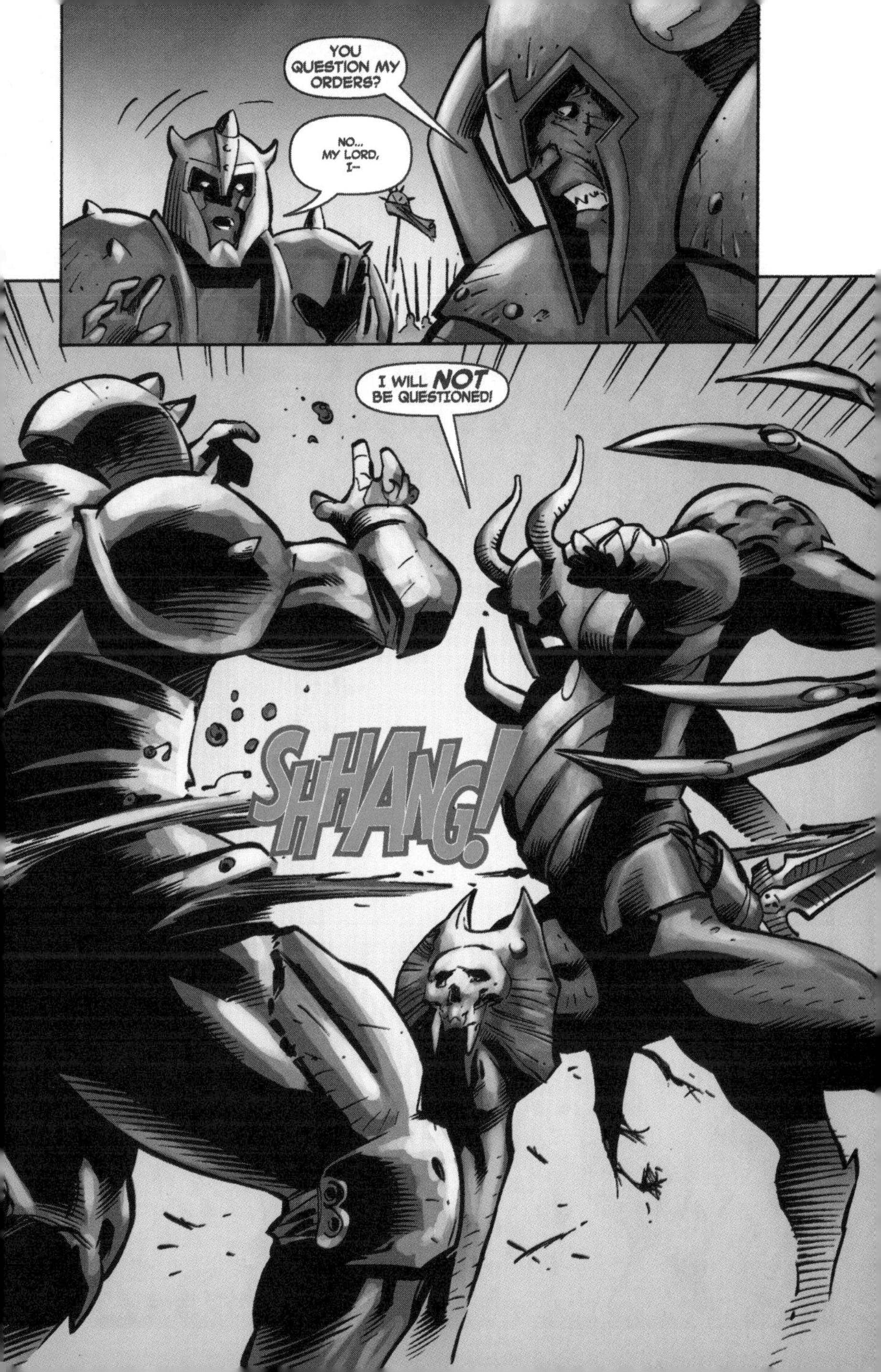
YOU QUESTION MY ORDERS?
NO... MY LORD, I--
I WILL NOT BE QUESTIONED!
SHHANG!

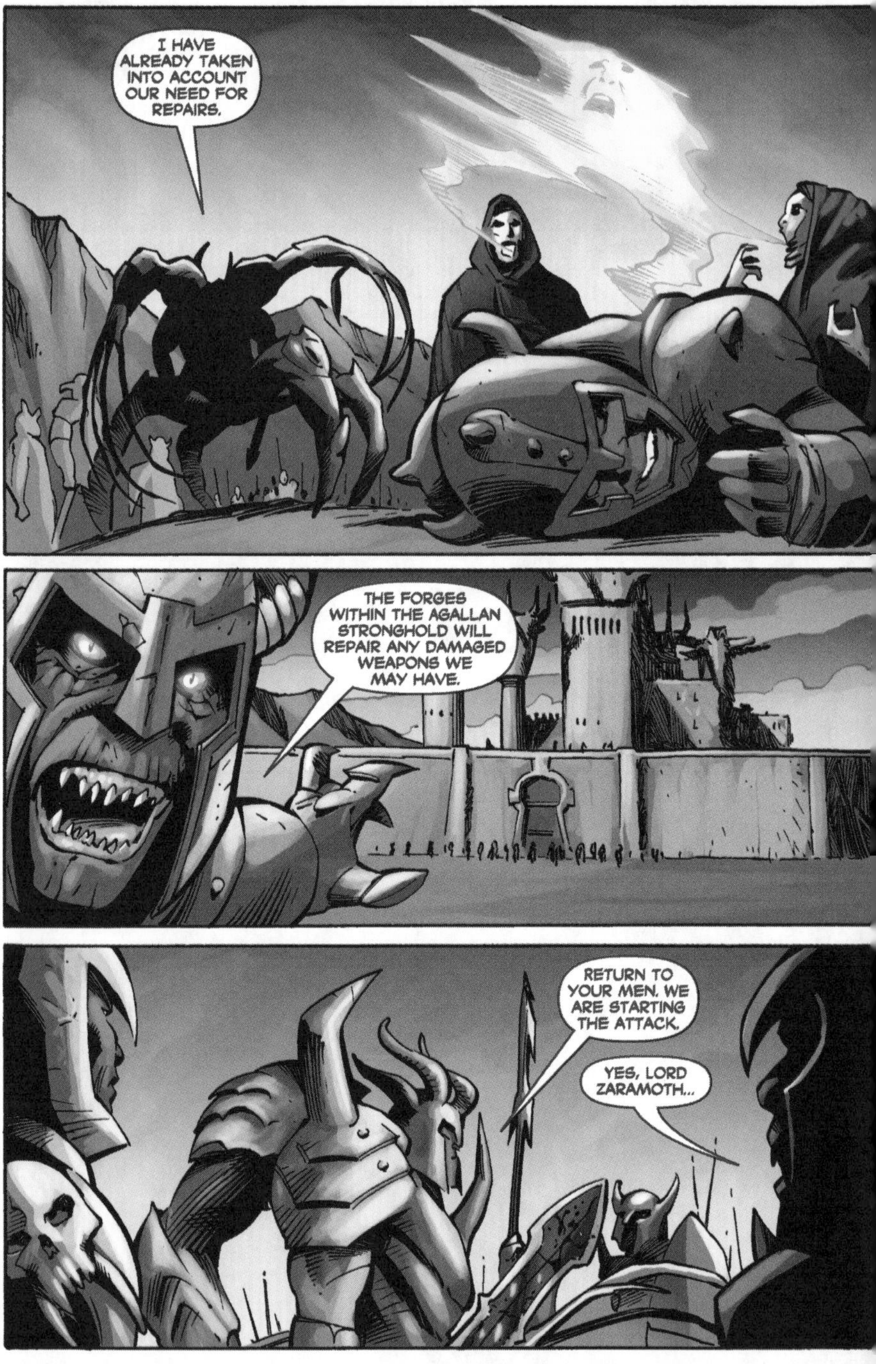
I HAVE ALREADY TAKEN INTO ACCOUNT OUR NEED FOR REPAIRS.
THE FORGES WITHIN THE AGALLAN STRONGHOLD WILL REPAIR ANY DAMAGED WEAPONS WE MAY HAVE.
RETURN TO YOUR MEN. WE ARE STARTING THE ATTACK.
YES, LORD ZARAMOTH...

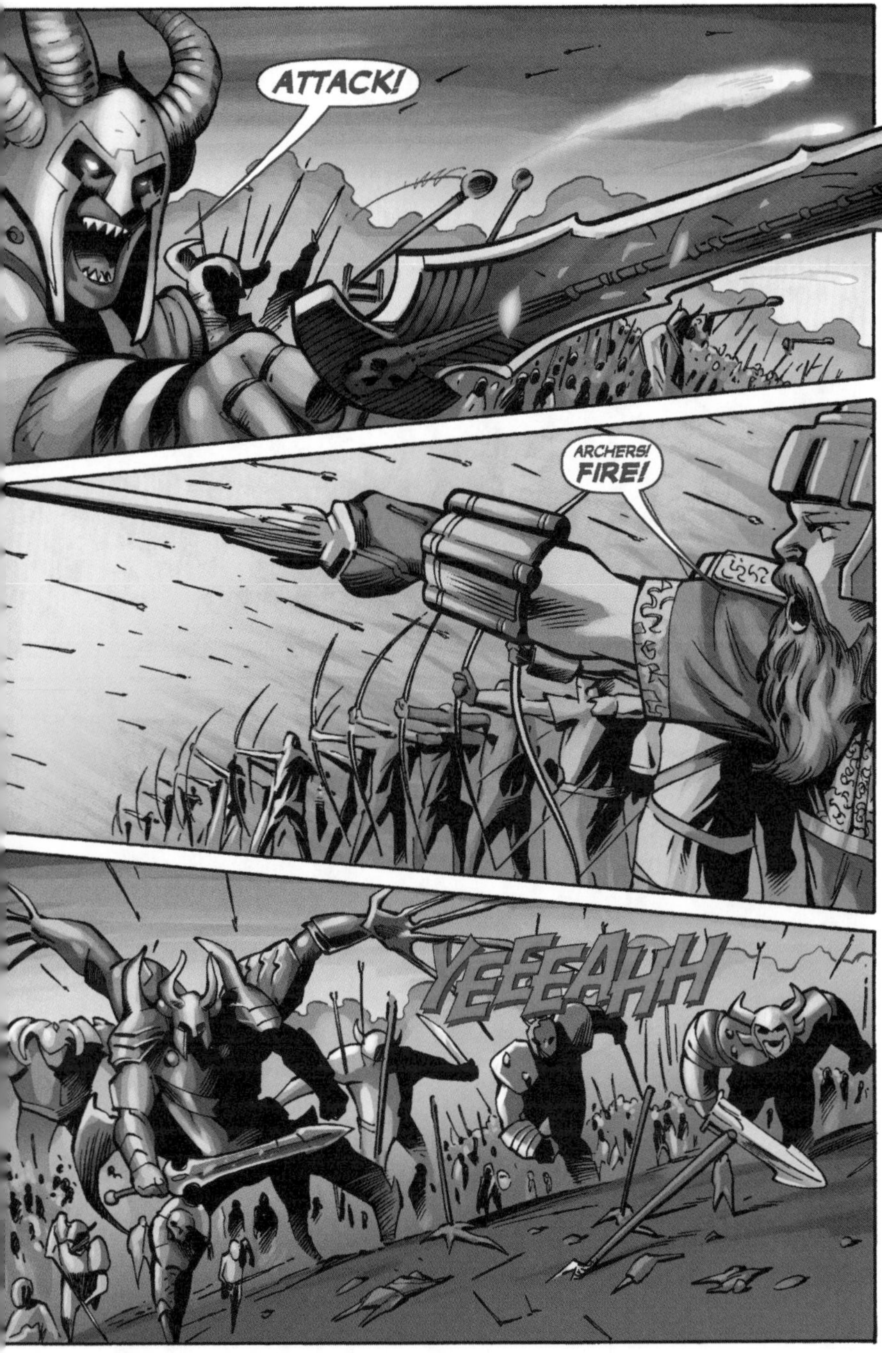
ATTACK!
ARCHERS! FIRE!
YEEEAHH

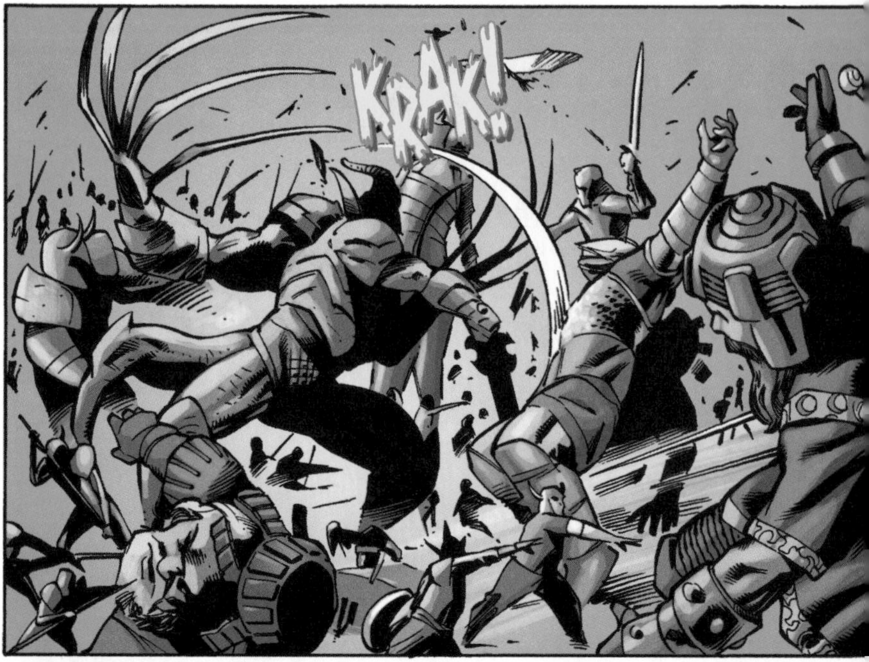
KRAK!

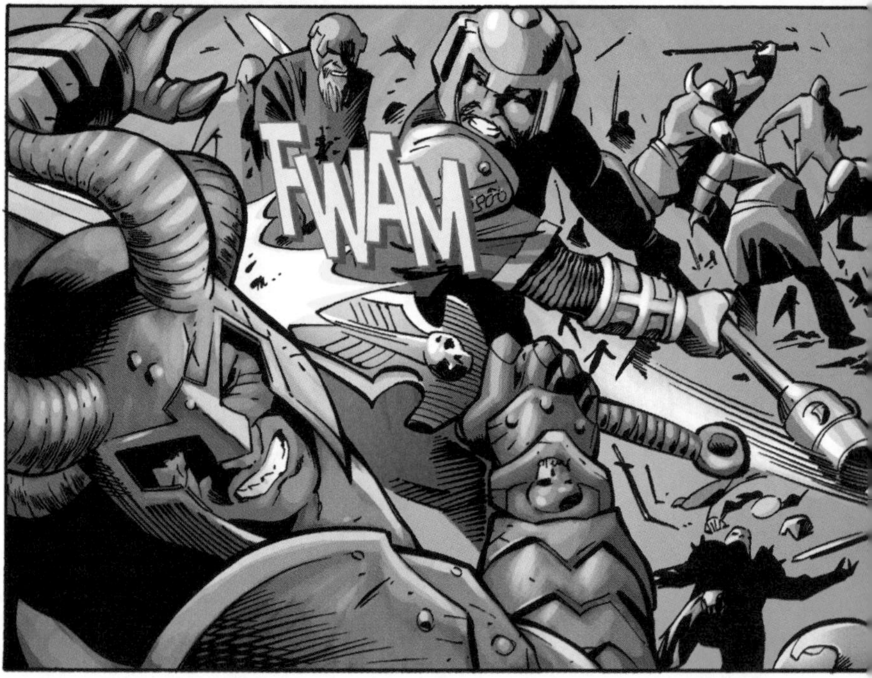
FWAM

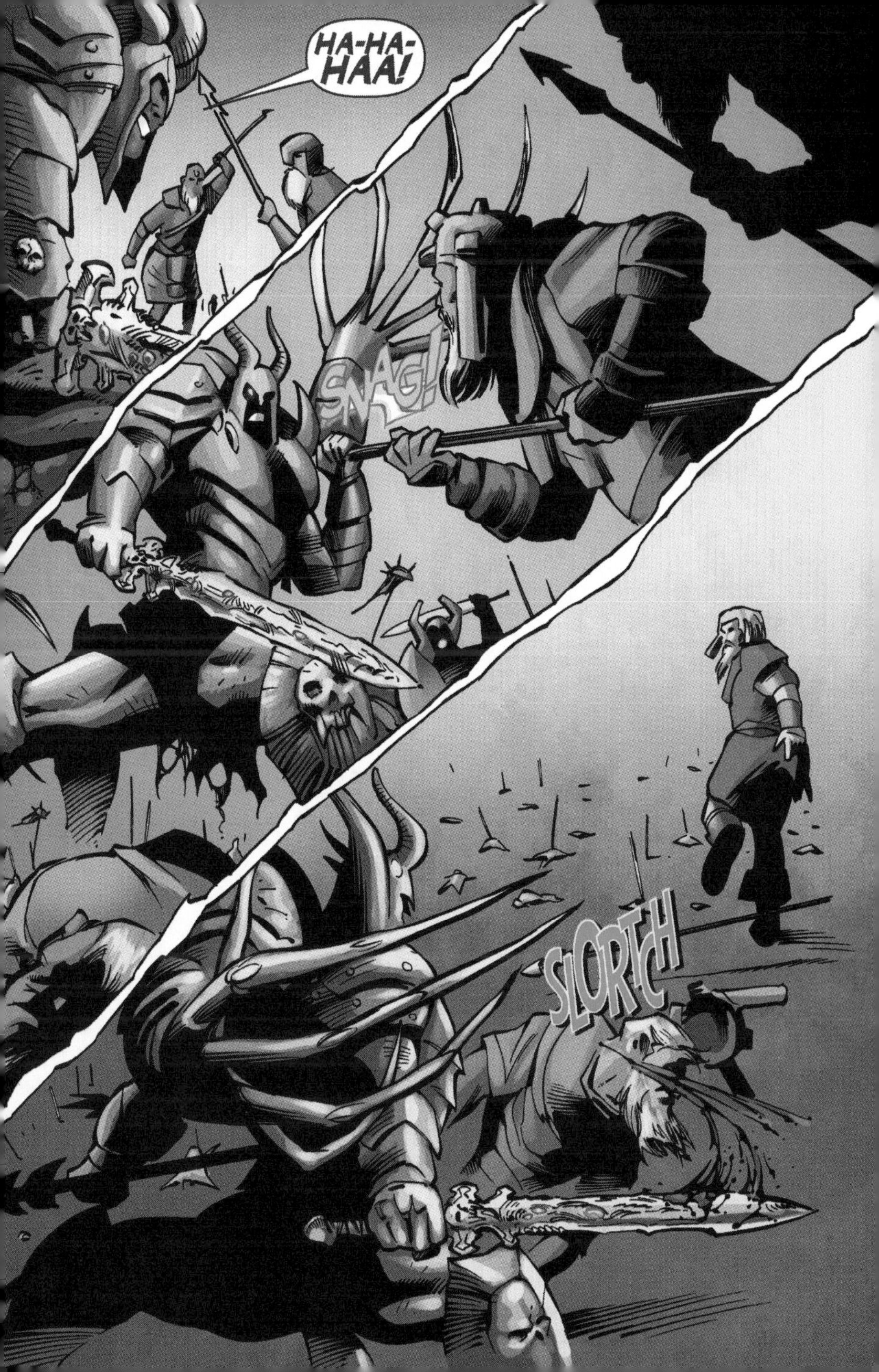
HA-HA-HAA!
SNAG!
SLORTCH

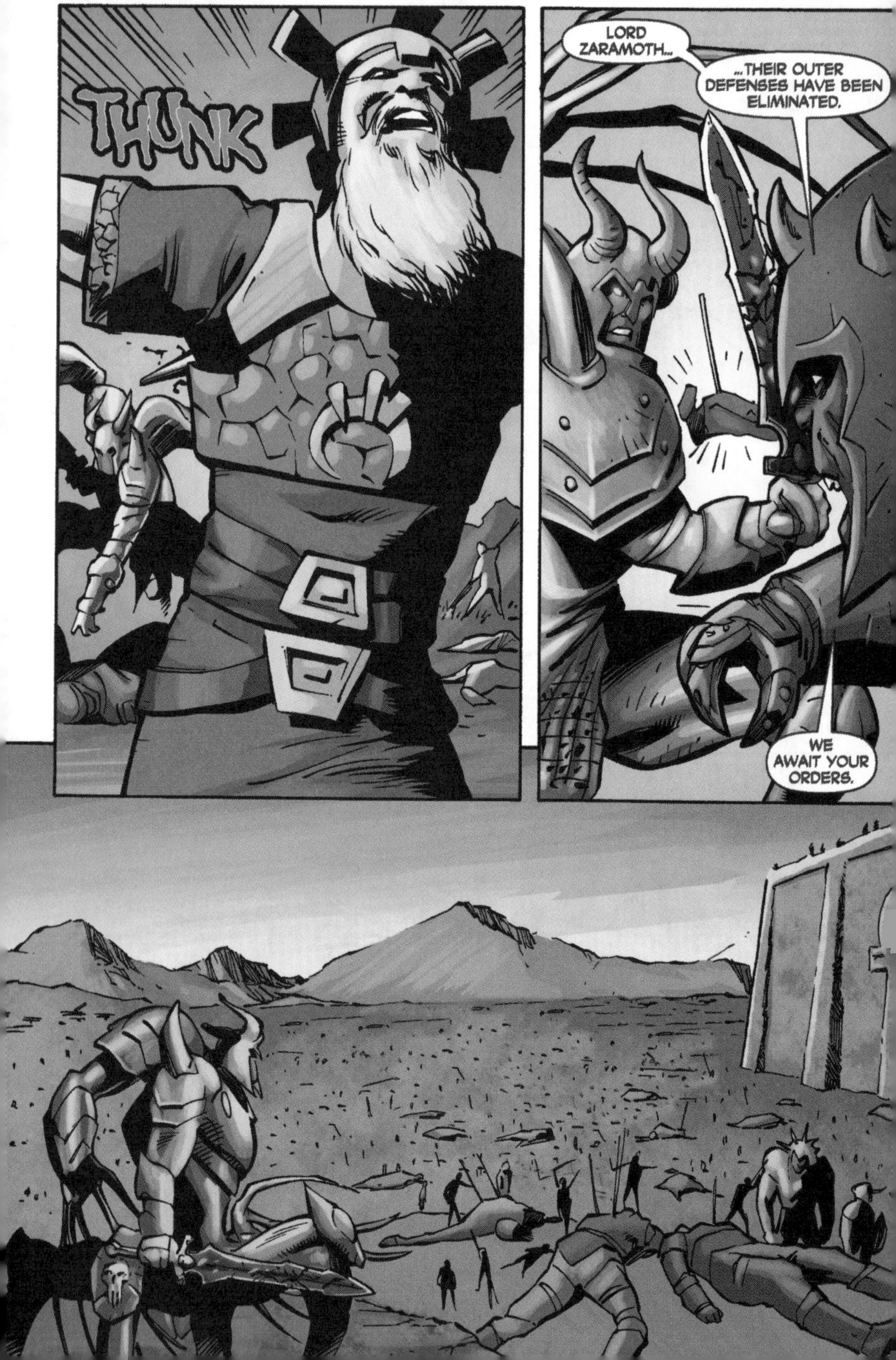
THUNK
LORD ZARAMOTH...
...THEIR OUTER DEFENSES HAVE BEEN ELIMINATED.
WE AWAIT YOUR ORDERS.

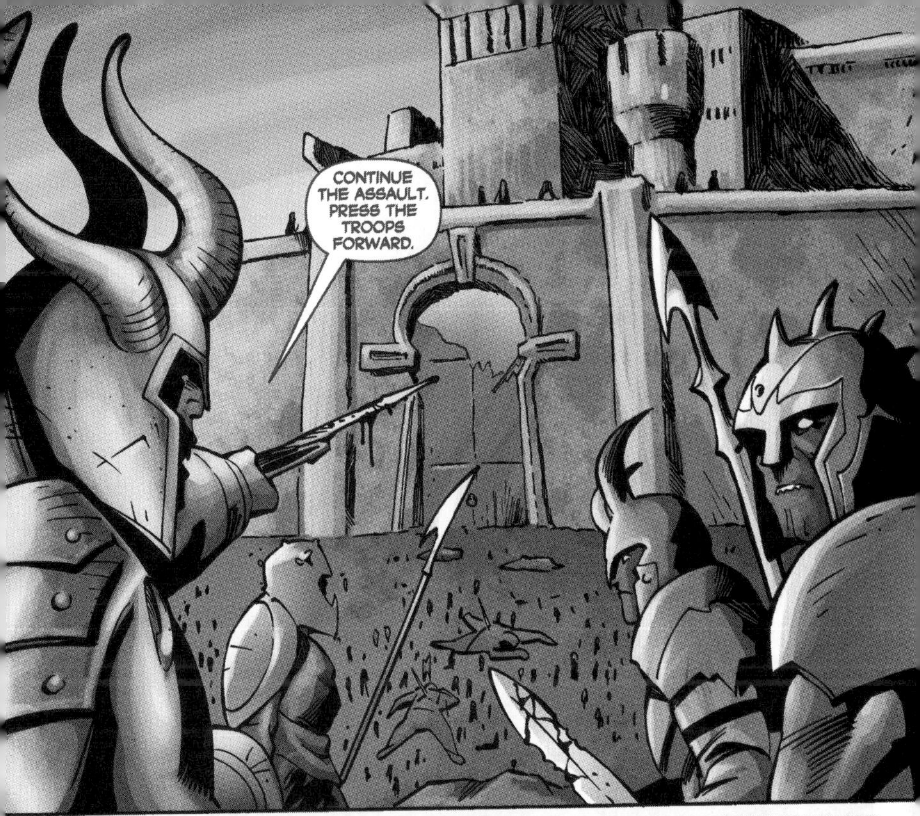
CONTINUE THE ASSAULT. PRESS THE TROOPS FORWARD.

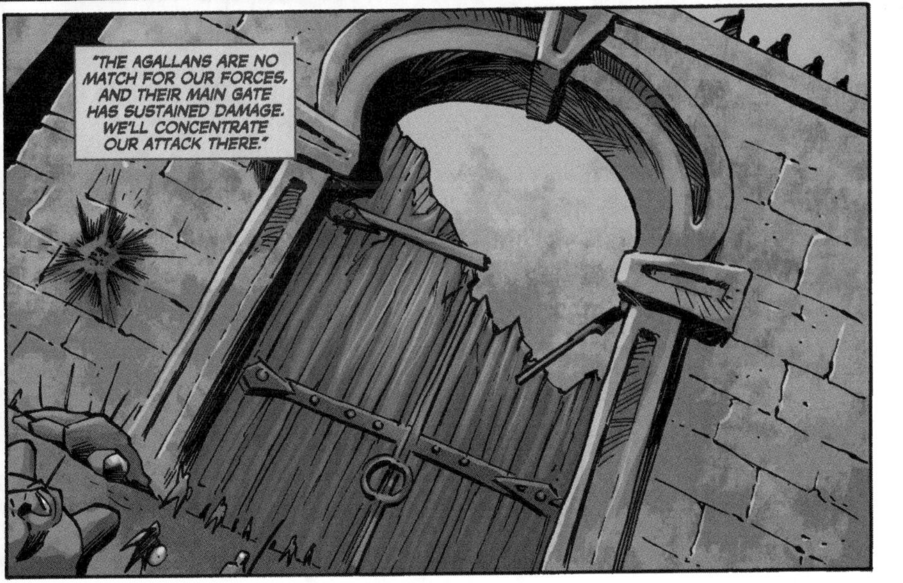
"THE AGALLANS ARE NO MATCH FOR OUR FORCES, AND THEIR MAIN GATE HAS SUSTAINED DAMAGE. WE'LL CONCENTRATE OUR ATTACK THERE."

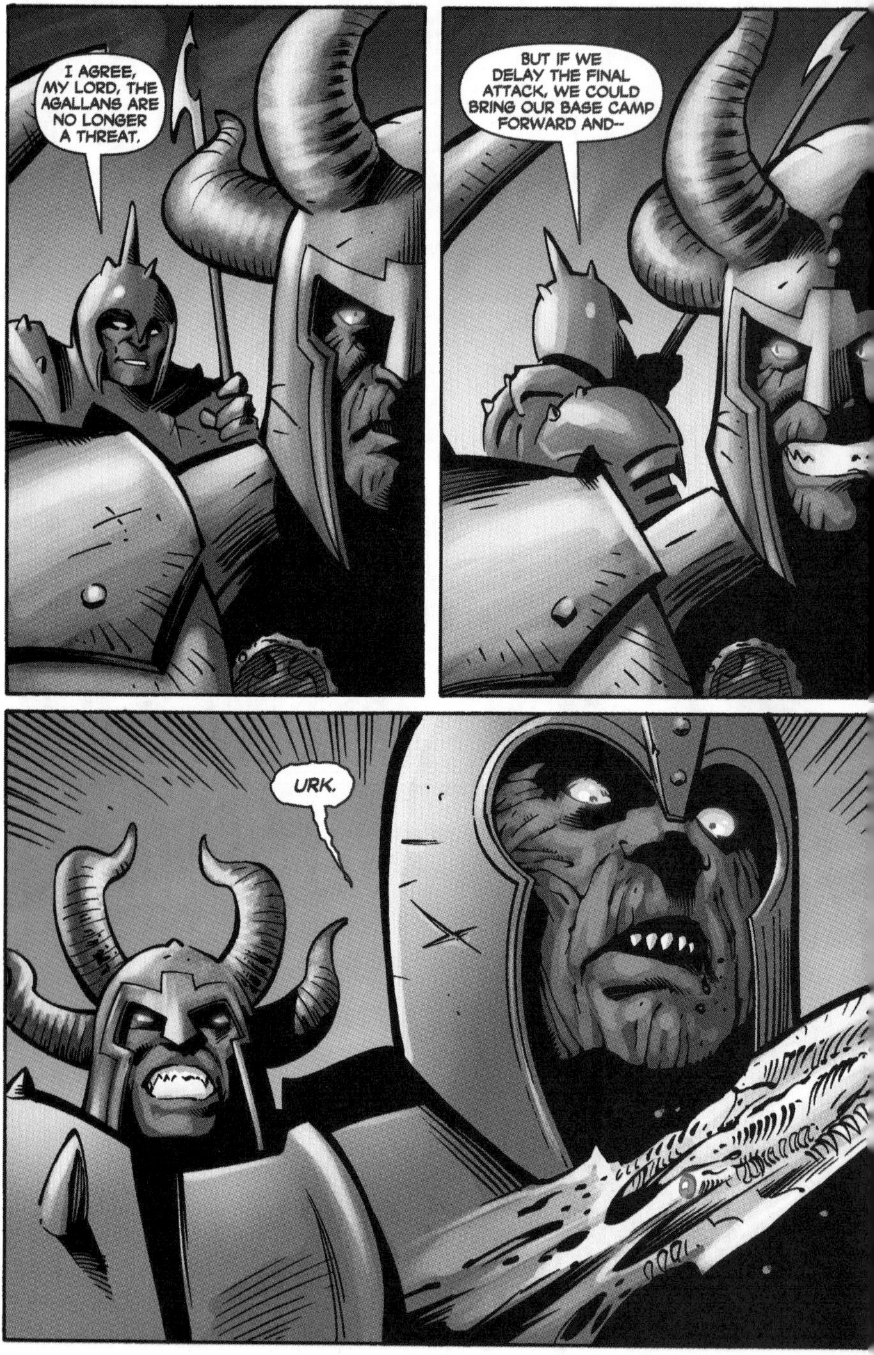
I AGREE, MY LORD, THE AGALLANS ARE NO LONGER A THREAT.
BUT IF WE DELAY THE FINAL ATTACK, WE COULD BRING OUR BASE CAMP FORWARD AND--
URK.

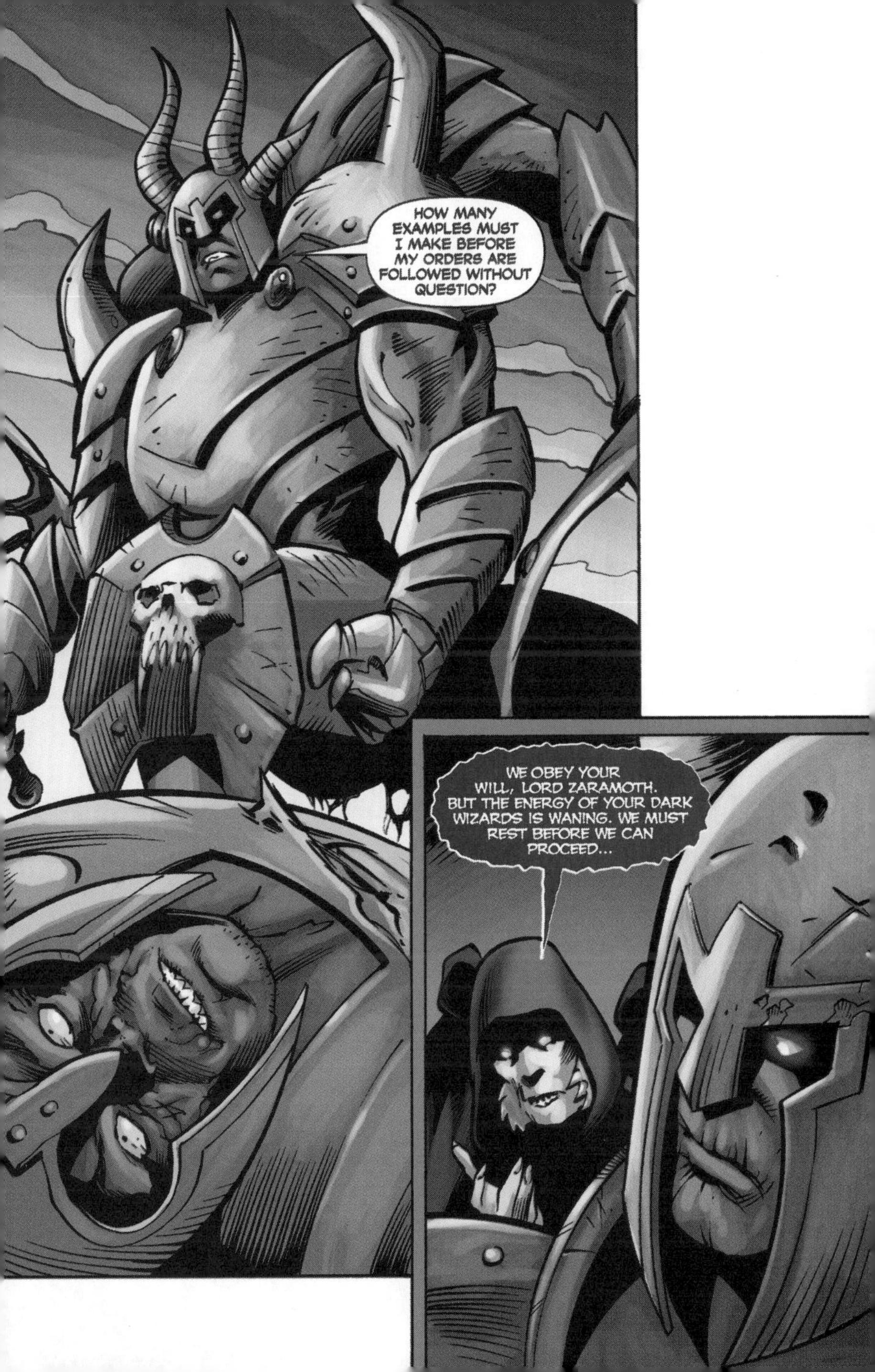
HOW MANY EXAMPLES MUST I MAKE BEFORE MY ORDERS ARE FOLLOWED WITHOUT QUESTION?
WE OBEY YOUR WILL, LORD ZARAMOTH. BUT THE ENERGY OF YOUR DARK WIZARDS IS WANING. WE MUST REST BEFORE WE CAN PROCEED...

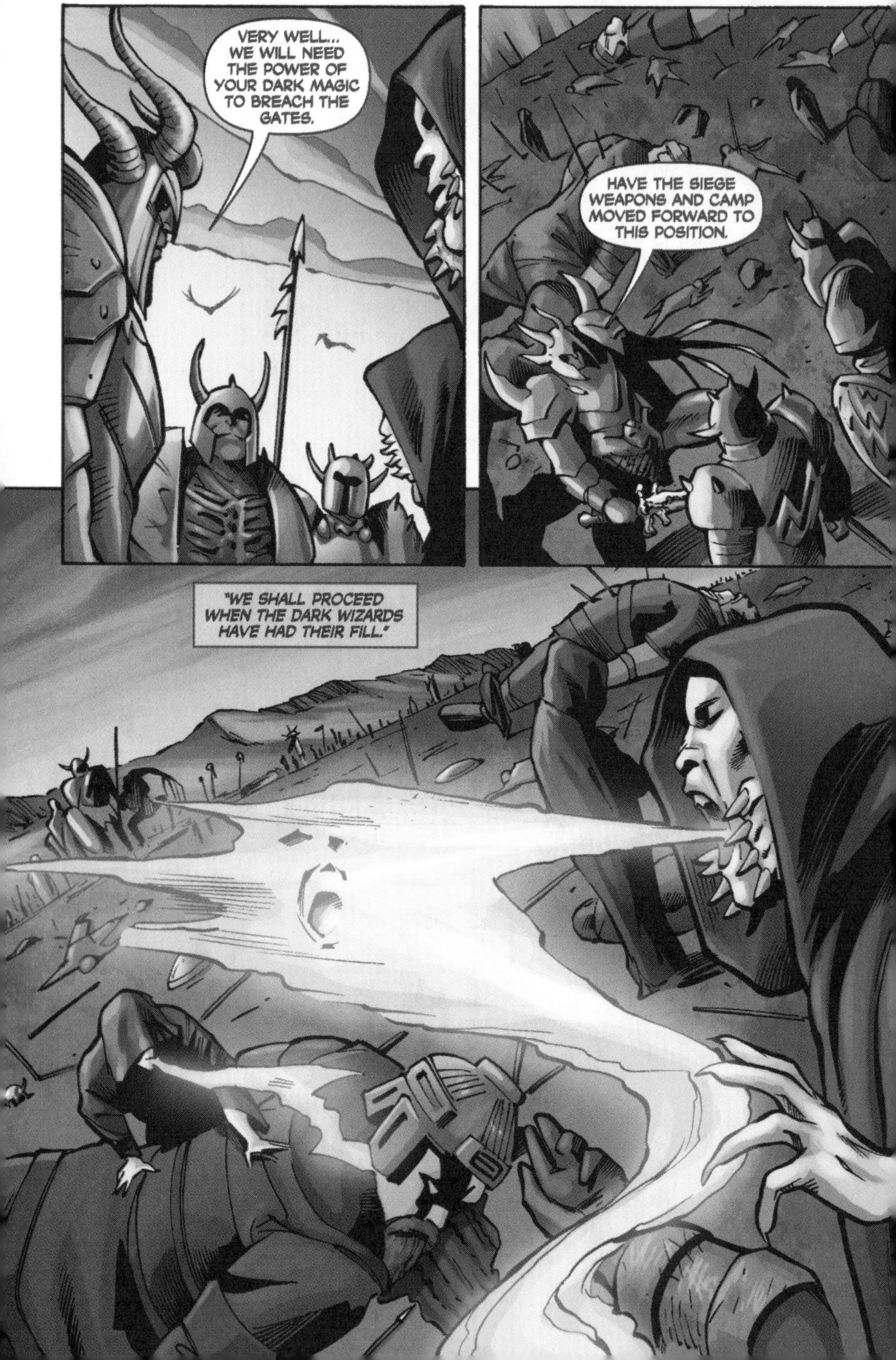
VERY WELL... WE WILL NEED THE POWER OF YOUR DARK MAGIC TO BREACH THE GATES.
HAVE THE SIEGE WEAPONS AND CAMP MOVED FORWARD TO THIS POSITION.
"WE SHALL PROCEED WHEN THE DARK WIZARDS HAVE HAD THEIR FILL."

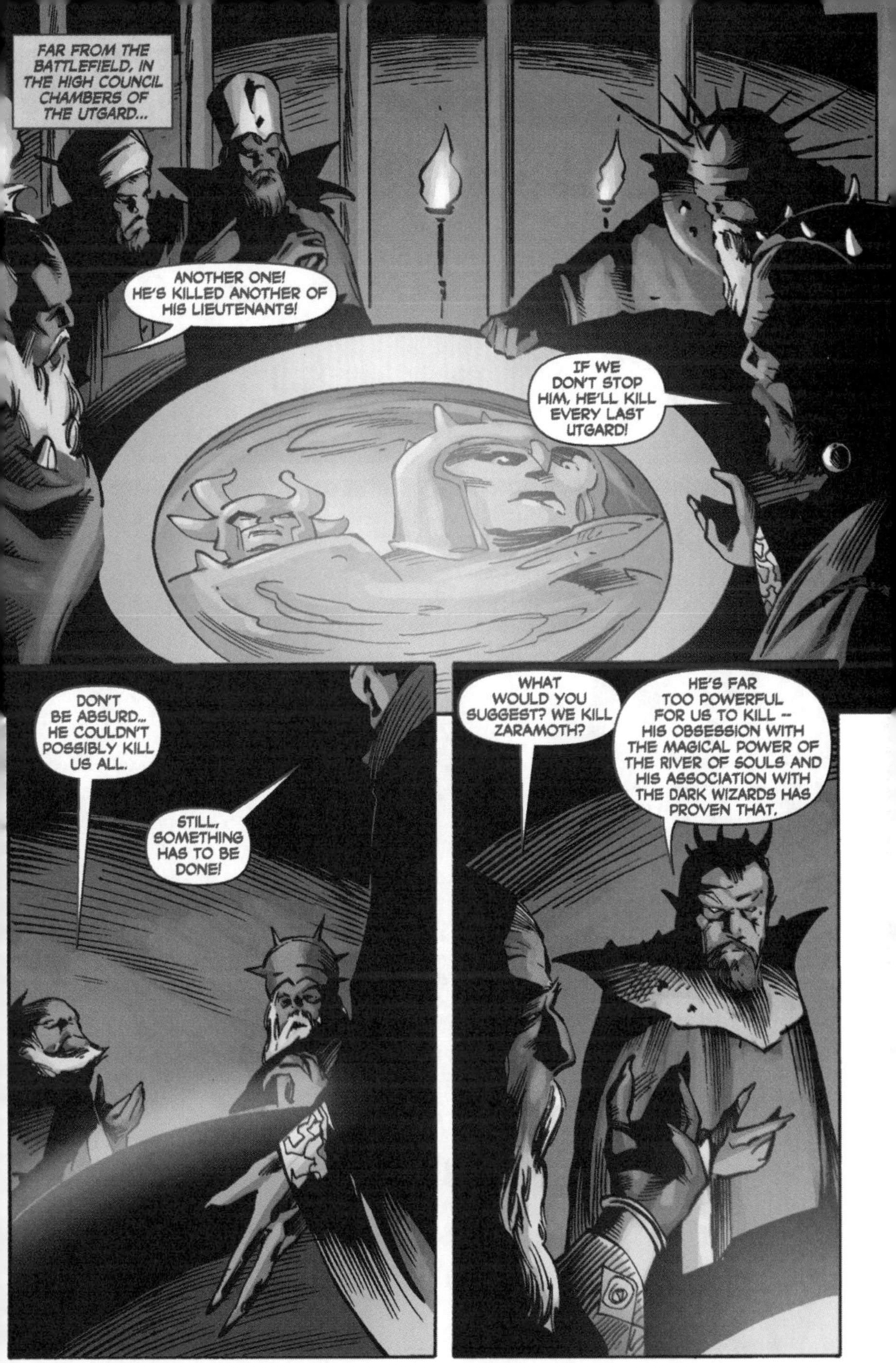
FAR FROM THE BATTLEFIELD, IN THE HIGH COUNCIL CHAMBERS OF THE UTGARD...
ANOTHER ONE! HE'S KILLED ANOTHER OF HIS LIEUTENANTS!
IF WE DON'T STOP HIM, HE'LL KILL EVERY LAST UTGARD!
DON'T BE ABSURD... HE COULDN'T POSSIBLY KILL US ALL.
STILL, SOMETHING HAS TO BE DONE!
WHAT WOULD YOU SUGGEST? WE KILL ZARAMOTH?
HE'S FAR TOO POWERFUL FOR US TO KILL -- HIS OBSESSION WITH THE MAGICAL POWER OF THE RIVER OF SOULS AND HIS ASSOCIATION WITH THE DARK WIZARDS HAS PROVEN THAT.

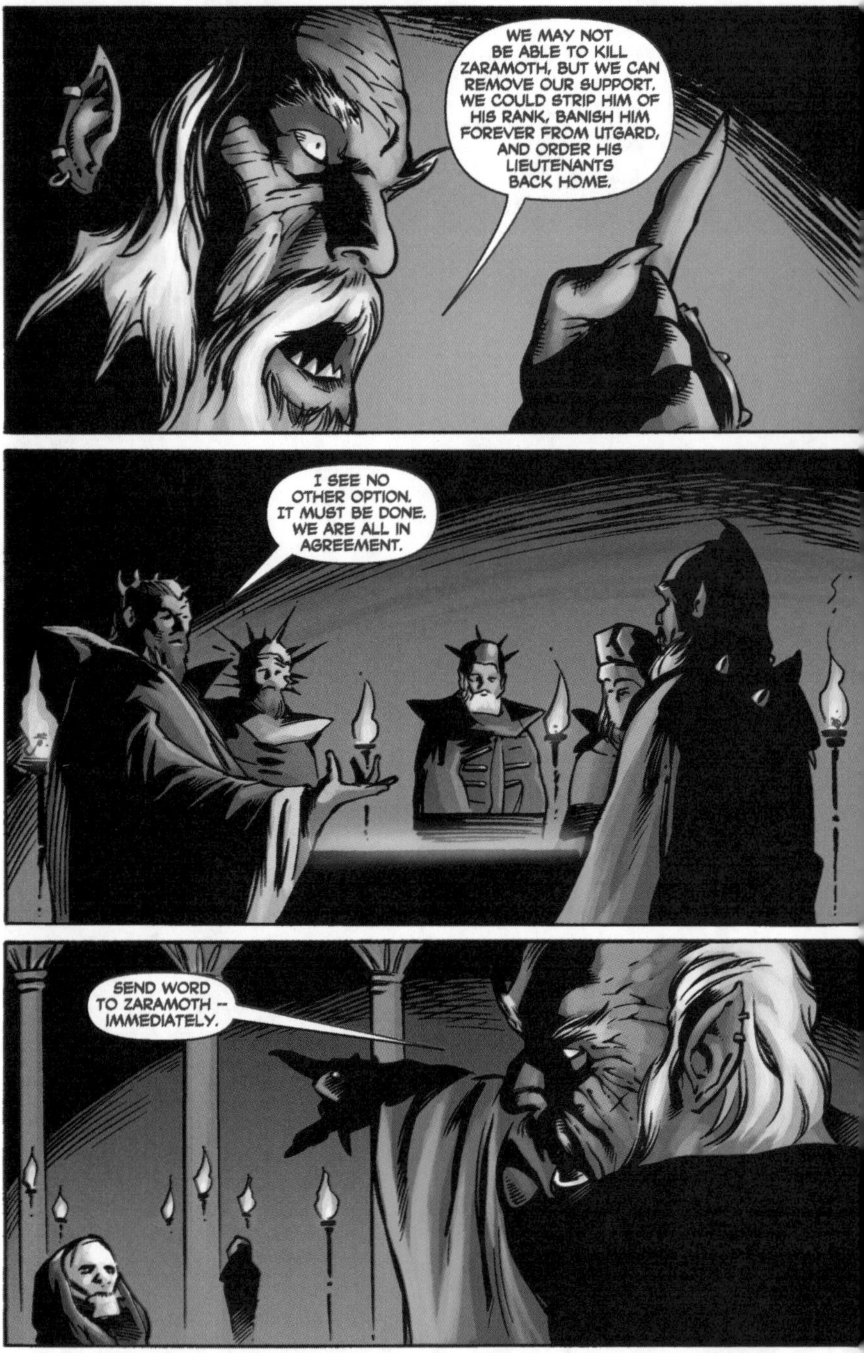
WE MAY NOT BE ABLE TO KILL ZARAMOTH, BUT WE CAN REMOVE OUR SUPPORT. WE COULD STRIP HIM OF HIS RANK, BANISH HIM FOREVER FROM UTGARD, AND ORDER HIS LIEUTENANTS BACK HOME.
I SEE NO OTHER OPTION. IT MUST BE DONE. WE ARE ALL IN AGREEMENT.
SEND WORD TO ZARAMOTH -- IMMEDIATELY.

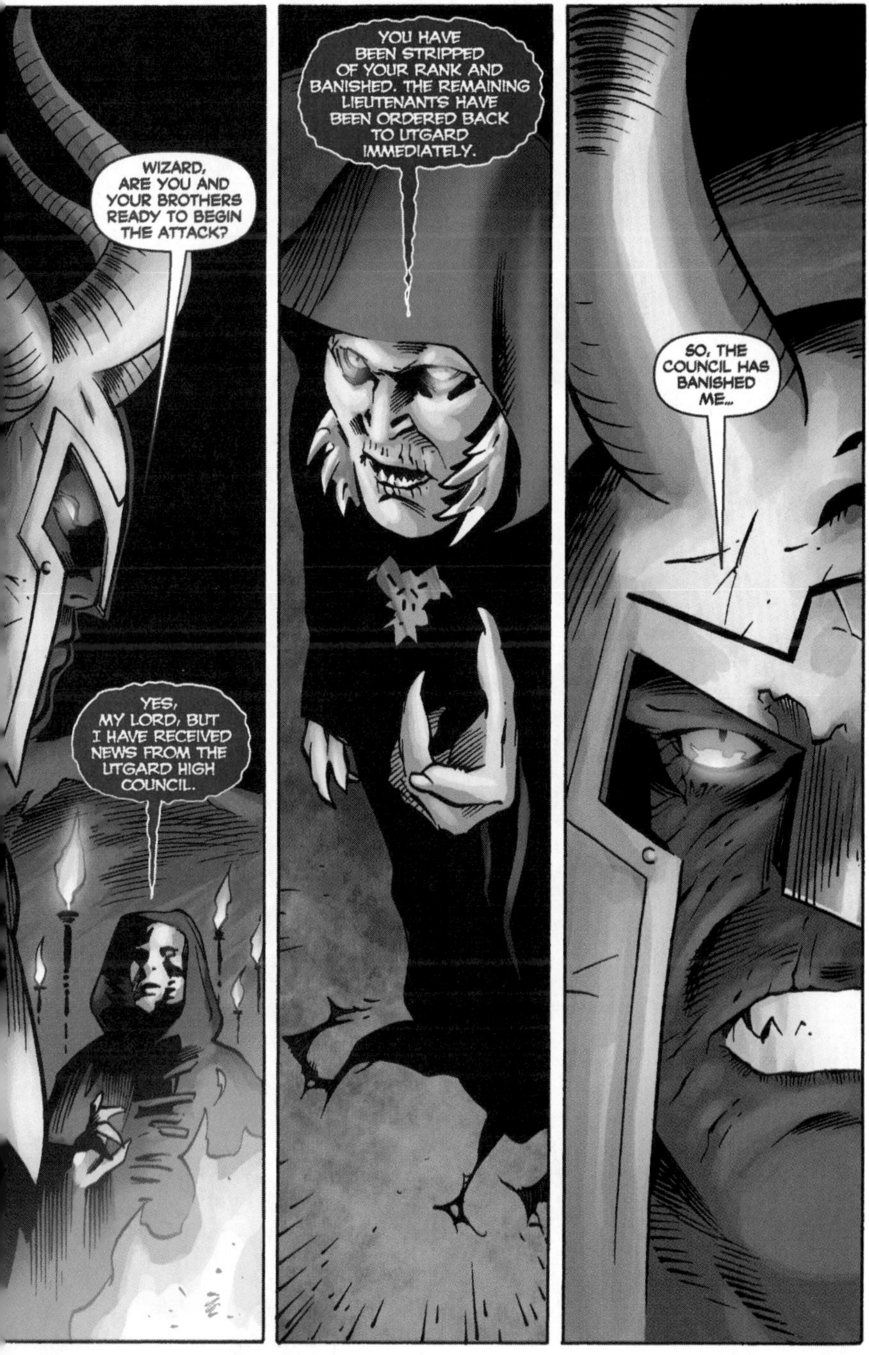
WIZARD, ARE YOU AND YOUR BROTHERS READY TO BEGIN THE ATTACK?
YES, MY LORD, BUT I HAVE RECEIVED NEWS FROM THE UTGARD HIGH COUNCIL.
YOU HAVE BEEN STRIPPED OF YOUR RANK AND BANISHED. THE REMAINING LIEUTENANTS HAVE BEEN ORDERED BACK TO UTGARD IMMEDIATELY.
SO, THE COUNCIL HAS BANISHED ME...

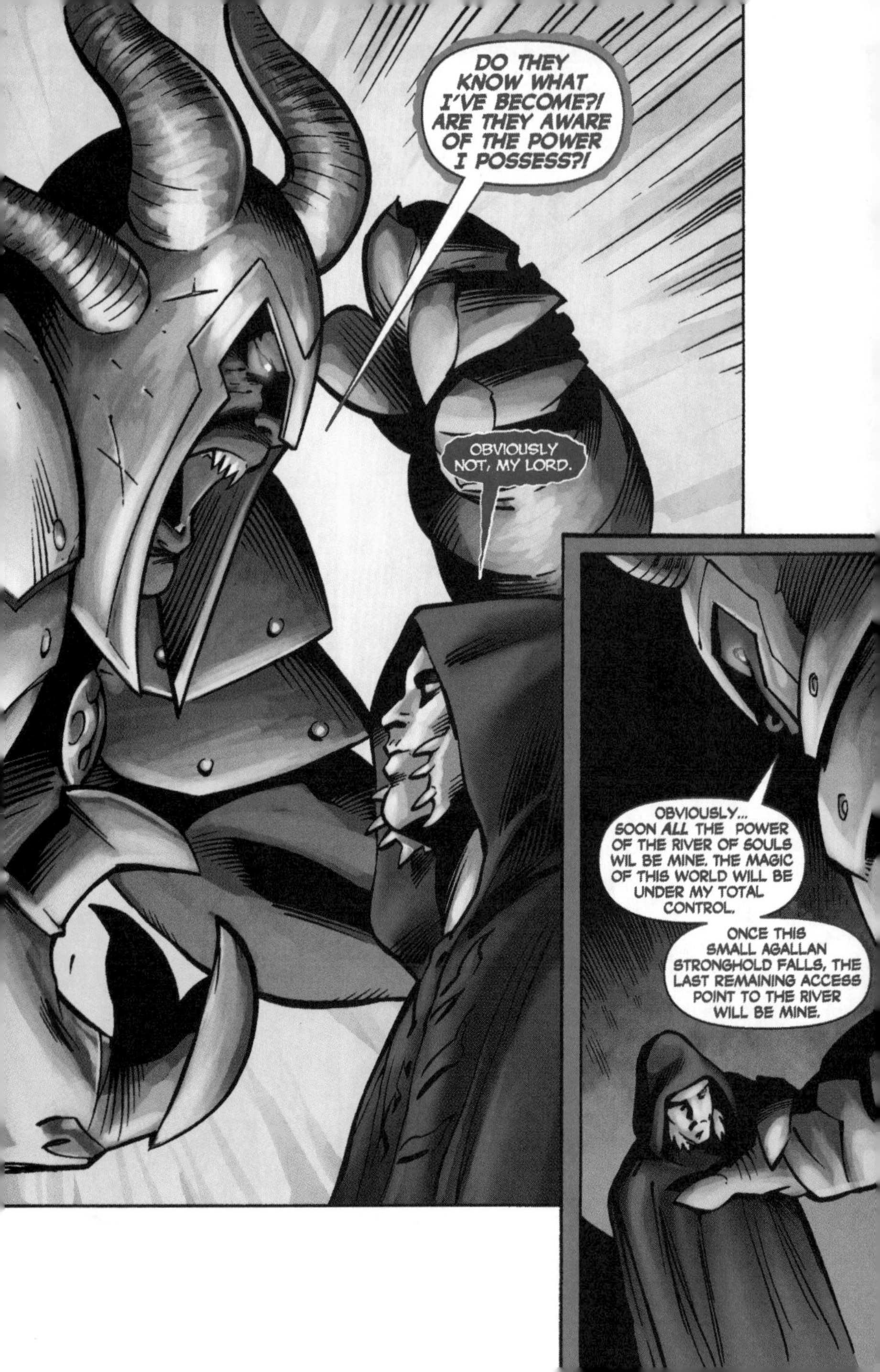
DO THEY KNOW WHAT I'VE BECOME?! ARE THEY AWARE OF THE POWER I POSSESS?!
OBVIOUSLY NOT, MY LORD.
OBVIOUSLY... SOON ALL THE POWER OF THE RIVER OF SOULS WIL BE MINE. THE MAGIC OF THIS WORLD WILL BE UNDER MY TOTAL CONTROL.
ONCE THIS SMALL AGALLAN STRONGHOLD FALLS, THE LAST REMAINING ACCESS POINT TO THE RIVER WILL BE MINE.

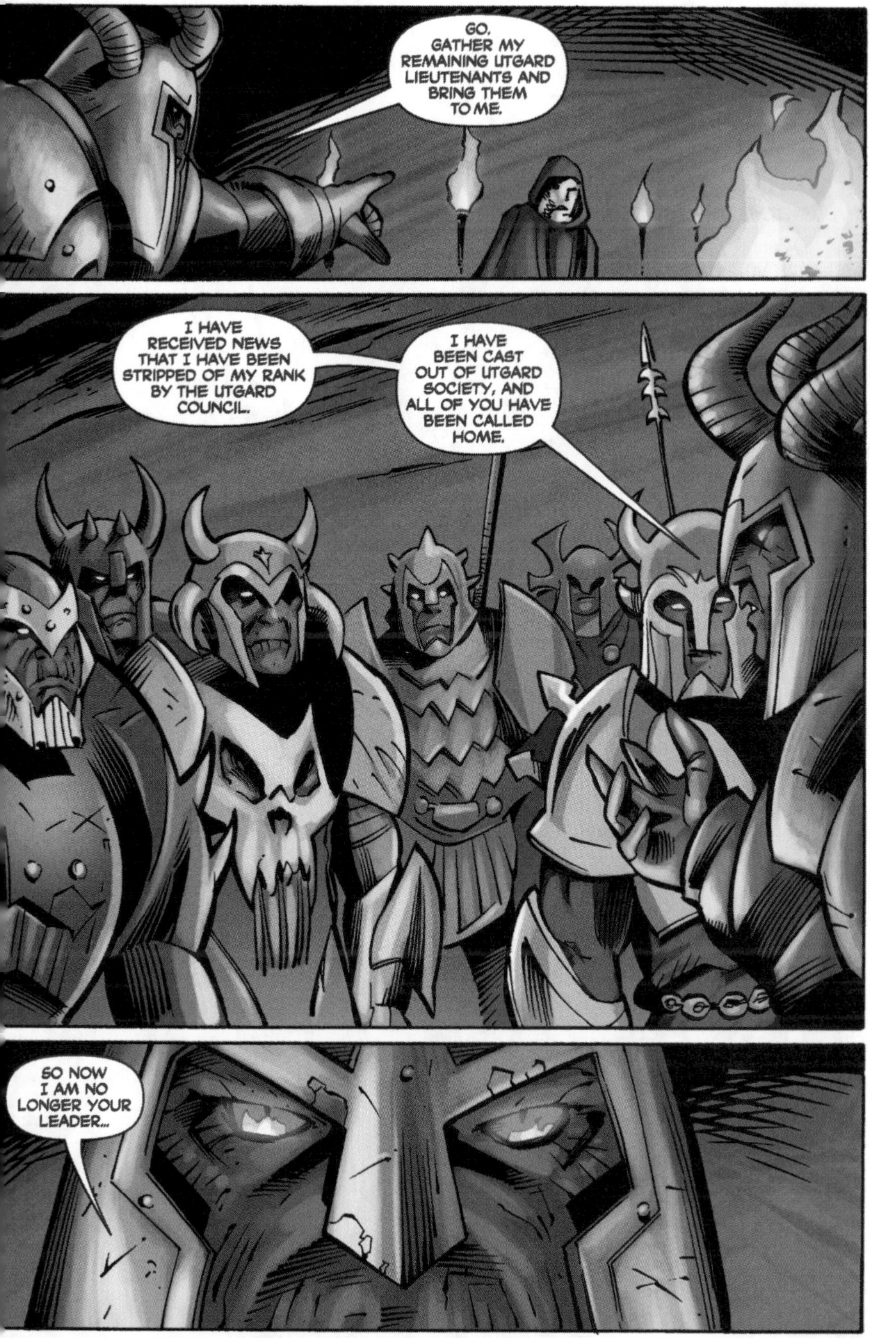
GO, GATHER MY REMAINING UTGARD LIEUTENANTS AND BRING THEM TO ME.
I HAVE RECEIVED NEWS THAT I HAVE BEEN STRIPPED OF MY RANK BY THE UTGARD COUNCIL.
I HAVE BEEN CAST OUT OF UTGARD SOCIETY, AND ALL OF YOU HAVE BEEN CALLED HOME.
SO NOW I AM NO LONGER YOUR LEADER...

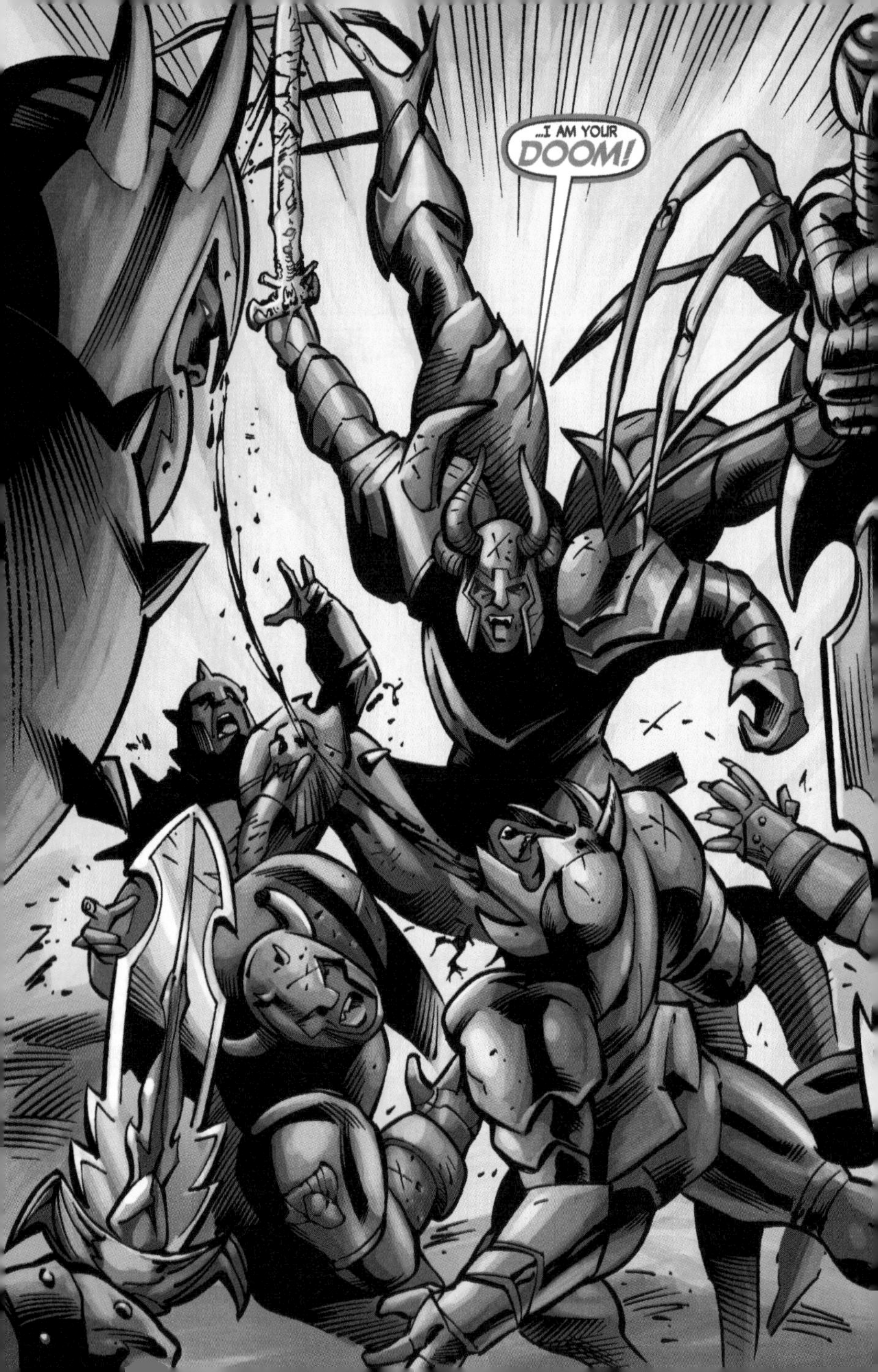
...I AM YOUR DOOM!

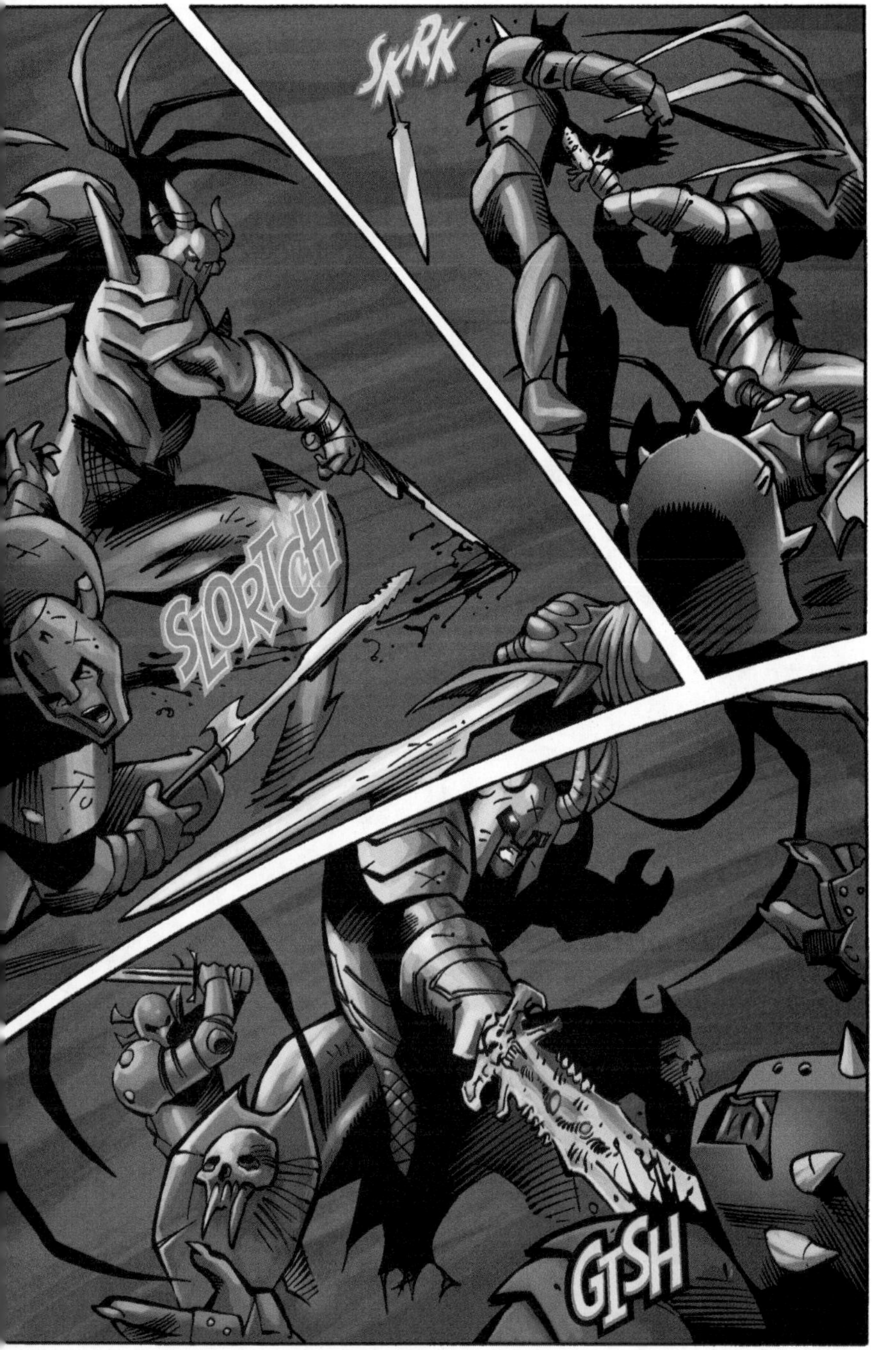
SKRK
SLORTCH
GISH

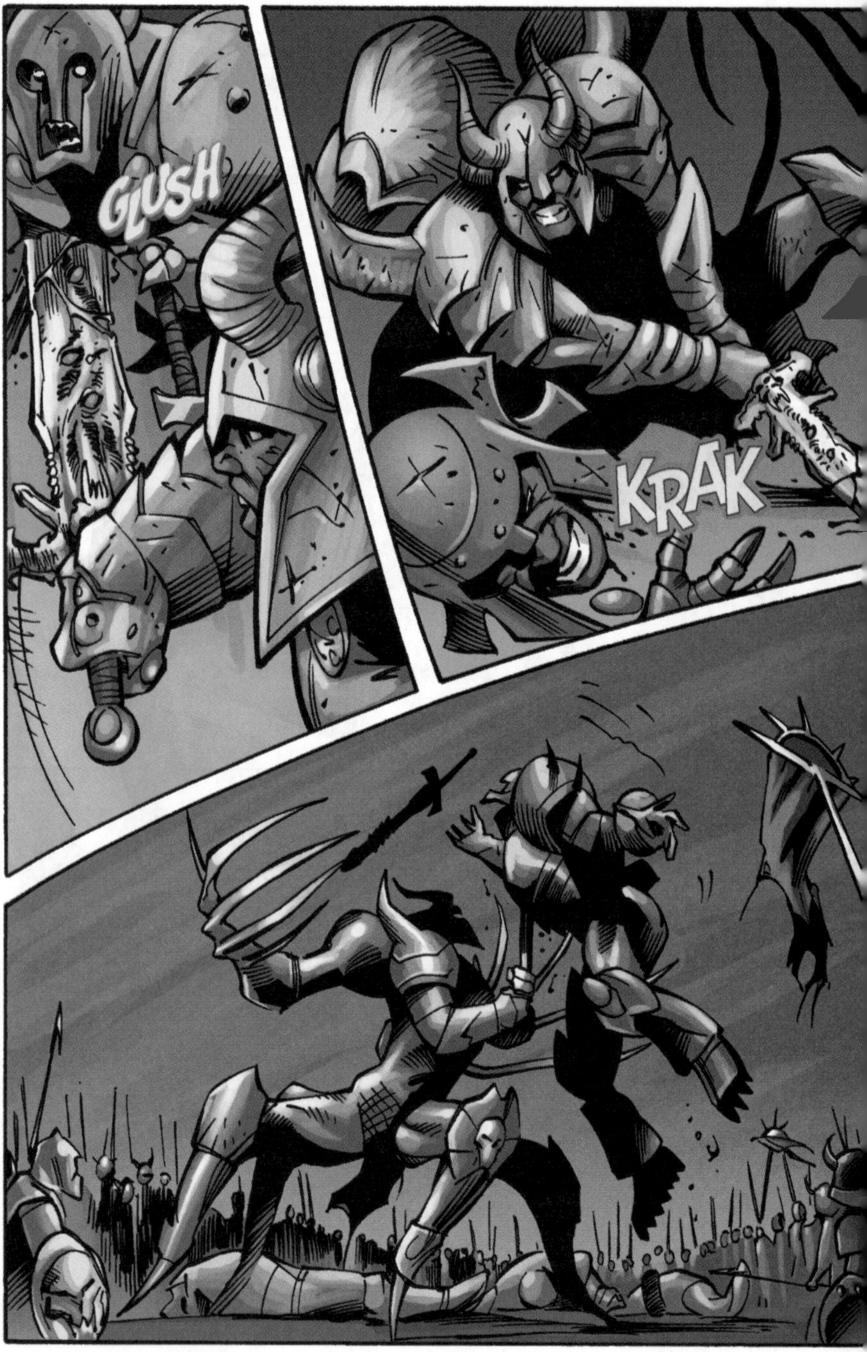
GLUSH
KRAK

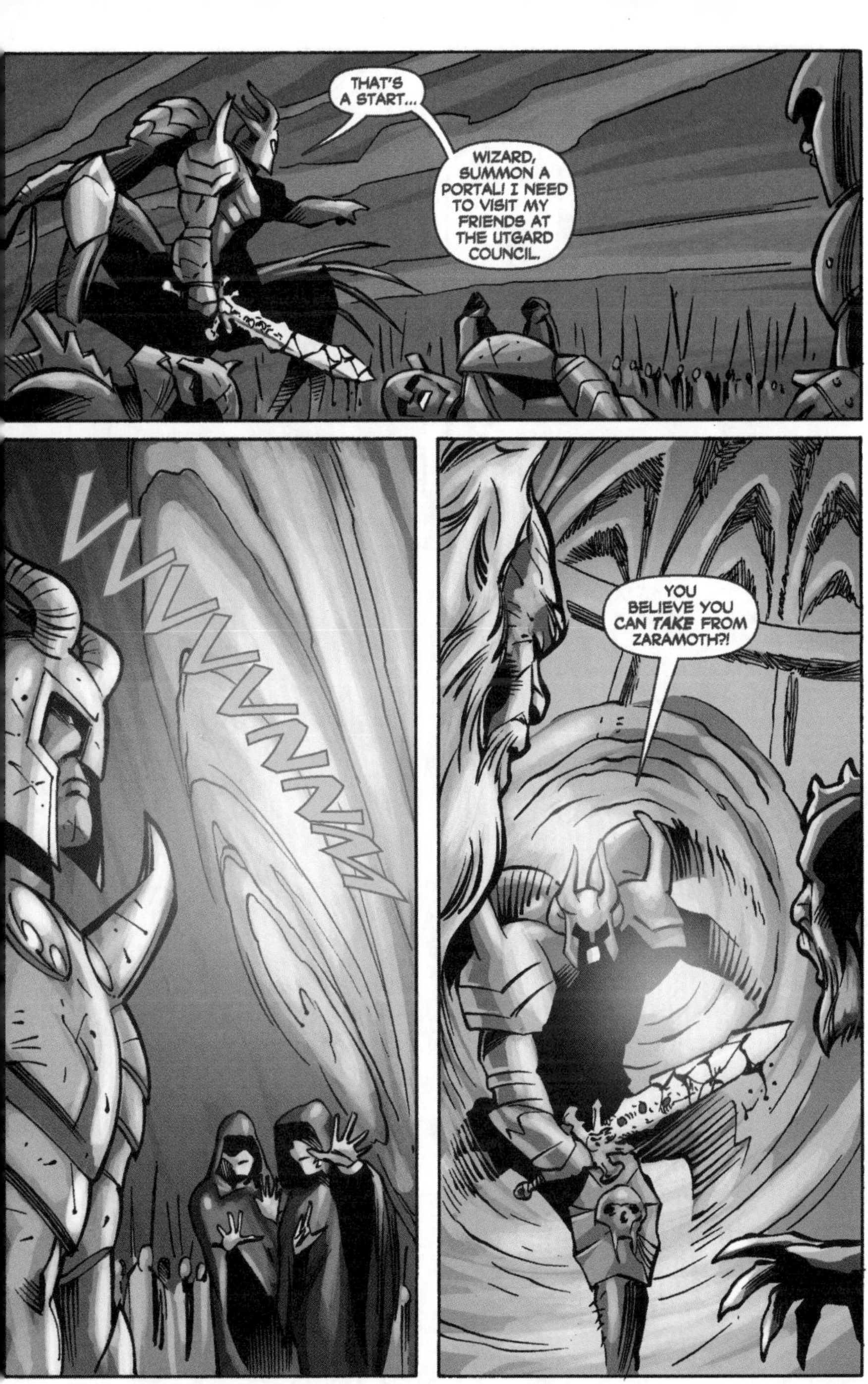
THAT'S A START...
WIZARD, SUMMON A PORTAL! I NEED TO VISIT MY FRIENDS AT THE UTGARD COUNCIL.
VVVVVNNNM
YOU BELIEVE YOU CAN *TAKE* FROM ZARAMOTH?!

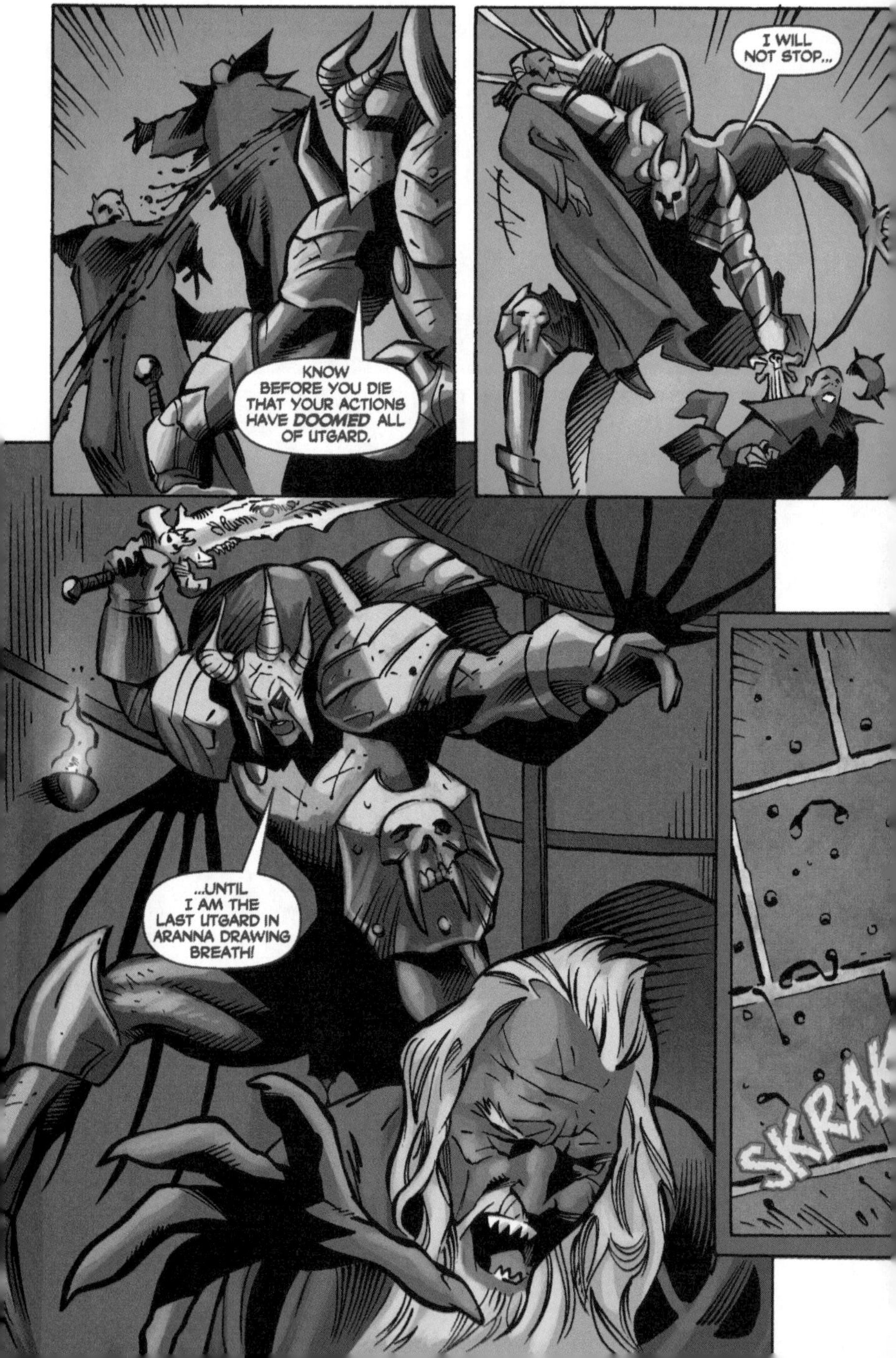
KNOW BEFORE YOU DIE THAT YOUR ACTIONS HAVE *DOOMED* ALL OF UTGARD.
I WILL NOT STOP...
...UNTIL I AM THE LAST UTGARD IN ARANNA DRAWING BREATH!
SKRAK

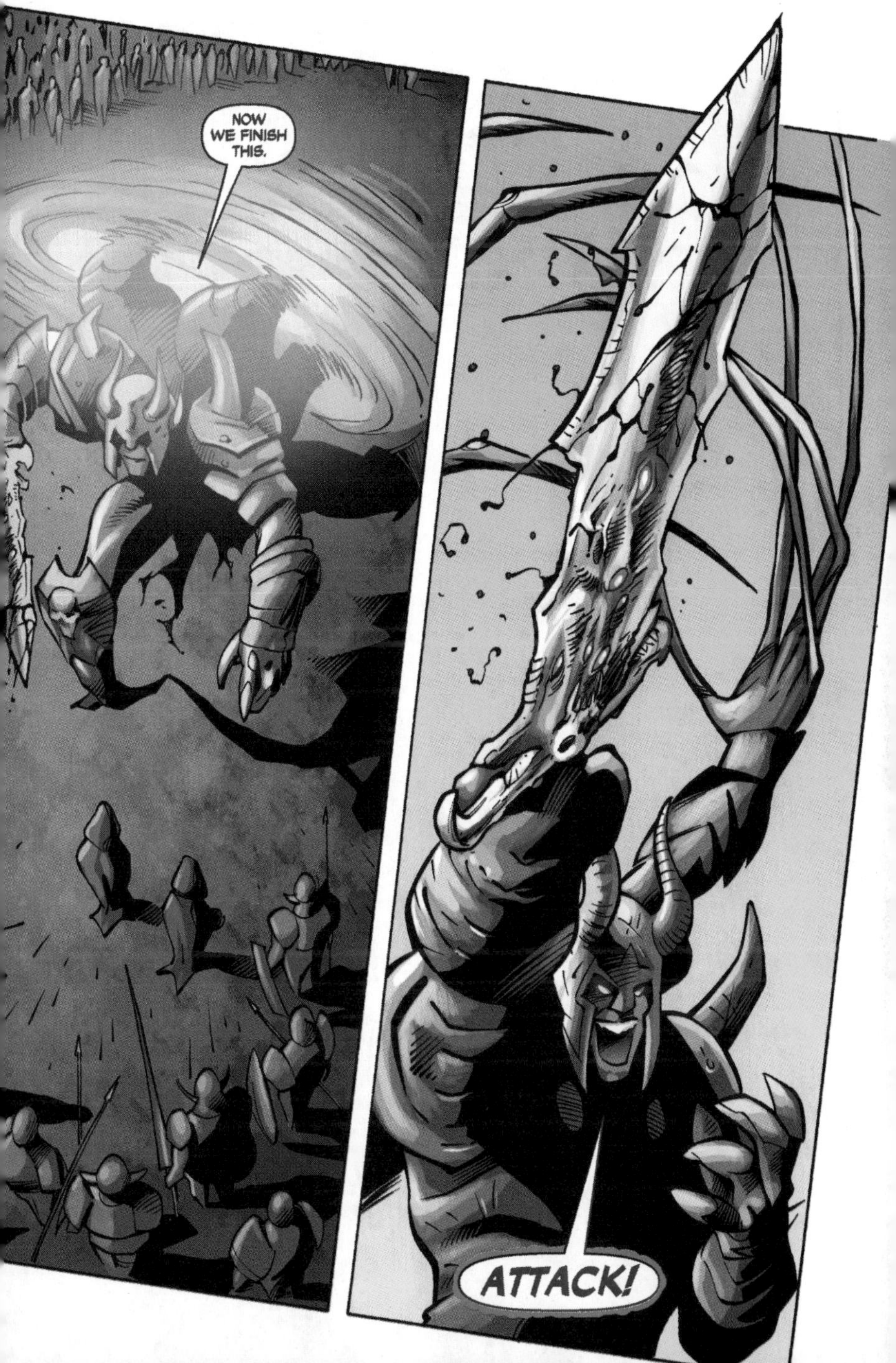
NOW WE FINISH THIS.
ATTACK!

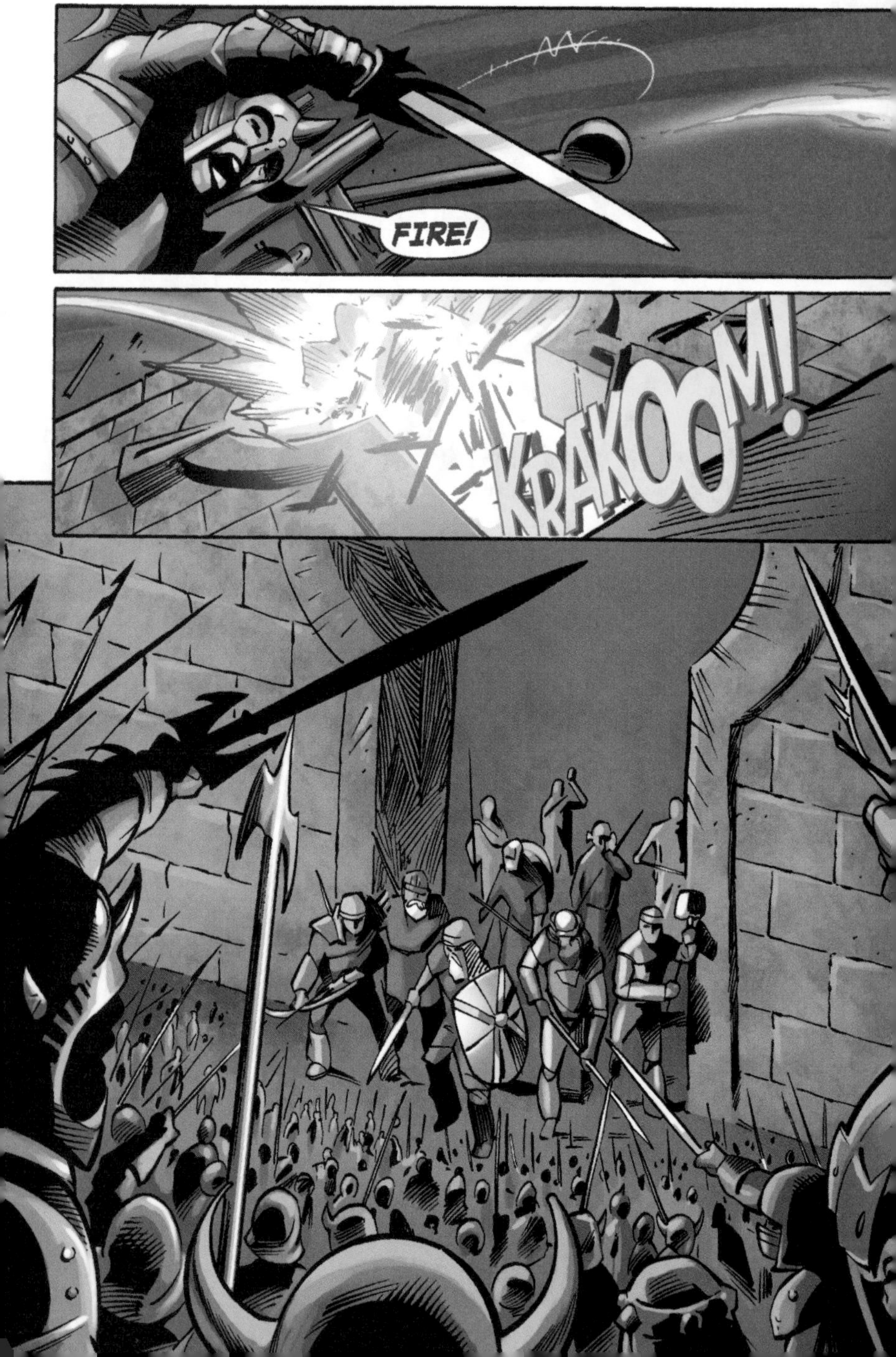
FIRE!
KRAKOOM!

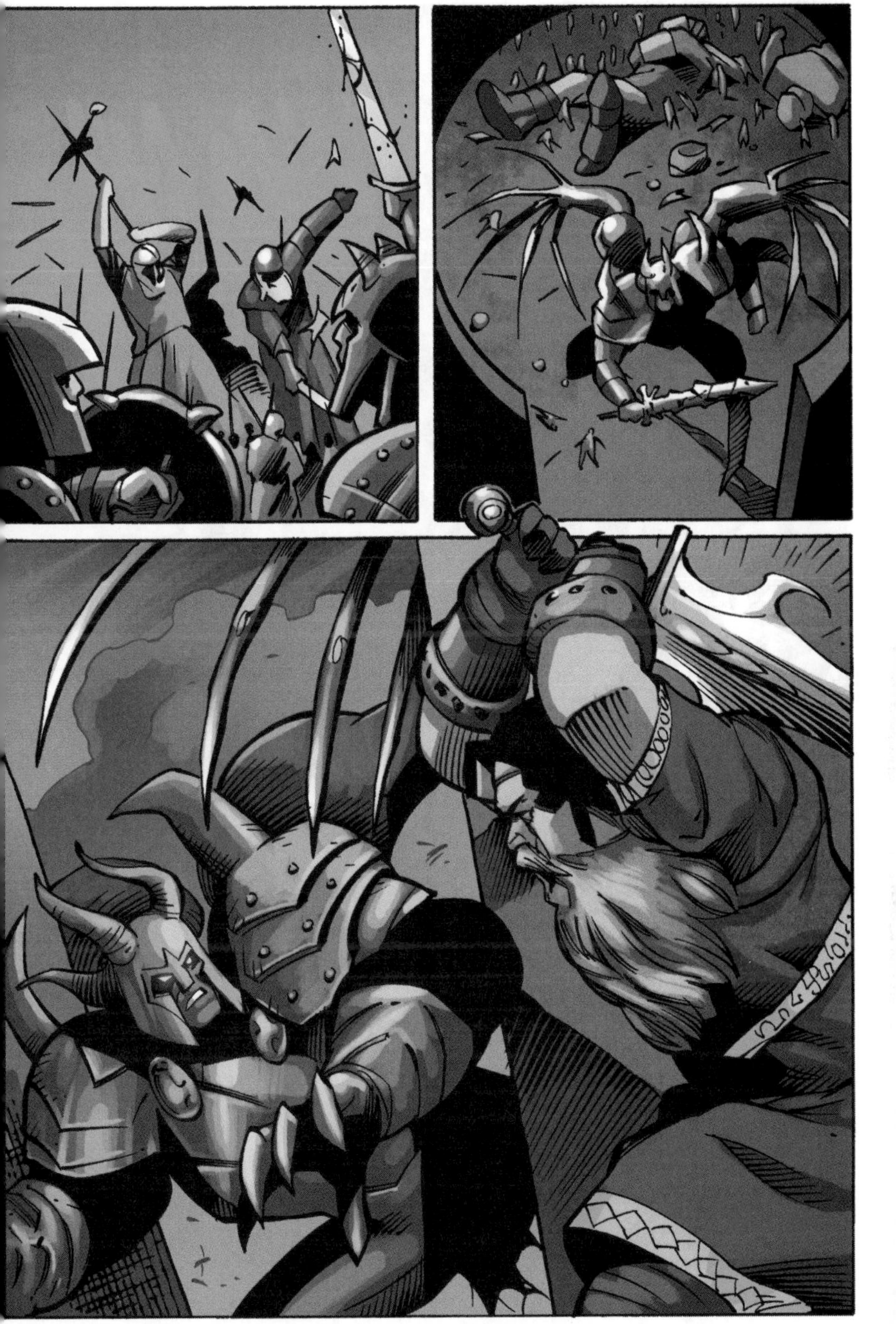

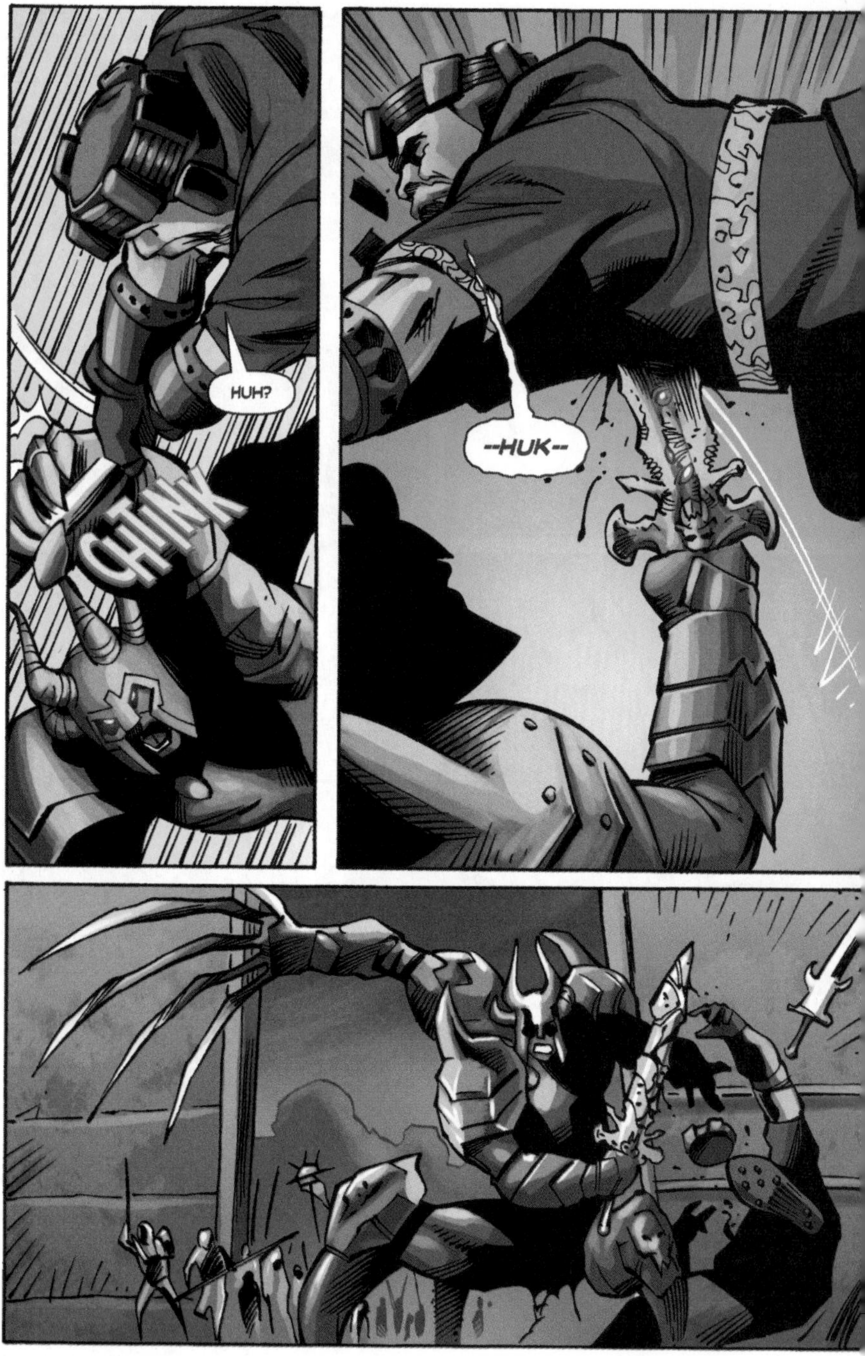
HUH?
CHINK
--HUK--

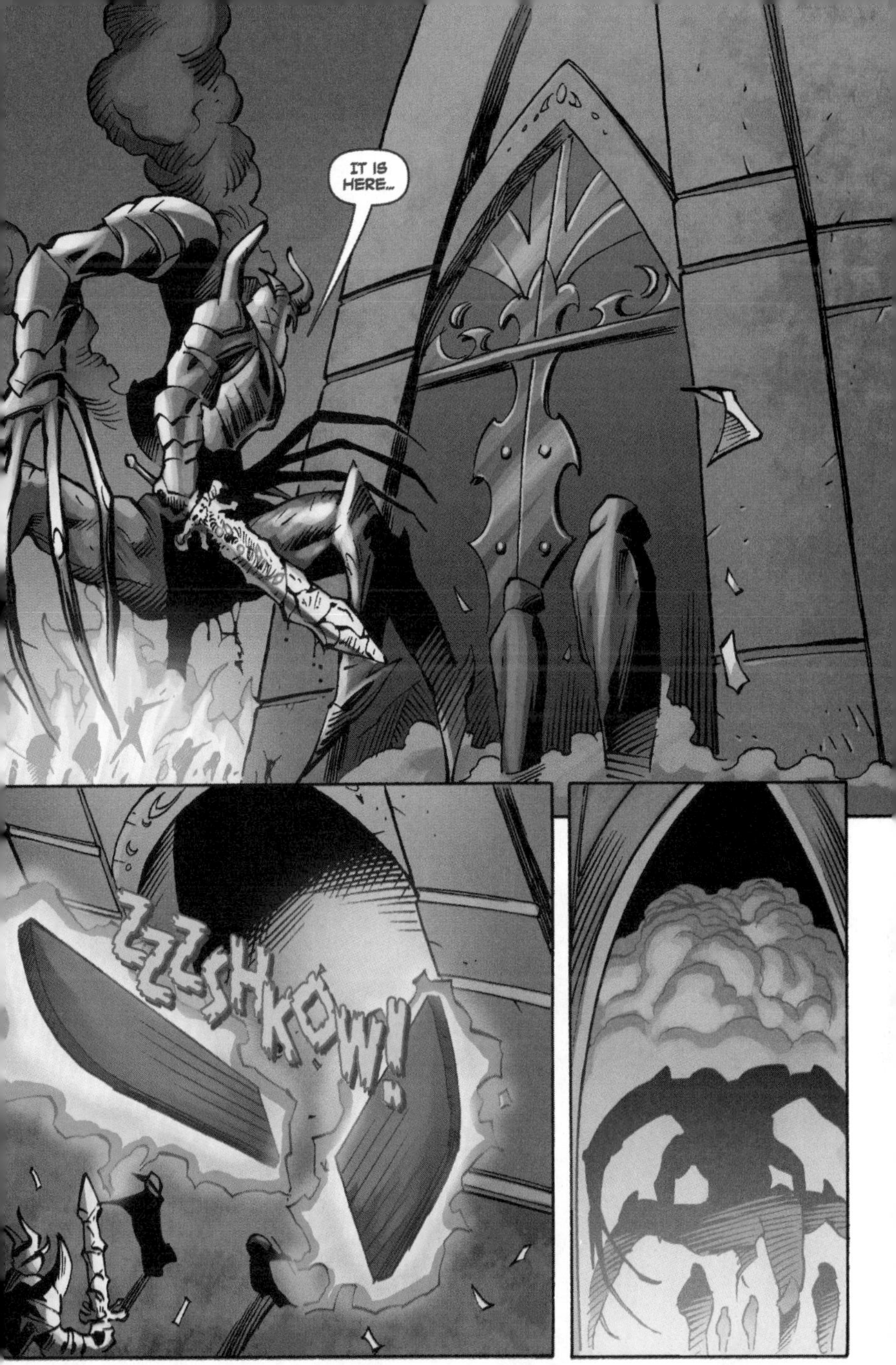
IT IS HERE...
ZZZSHKOW!!

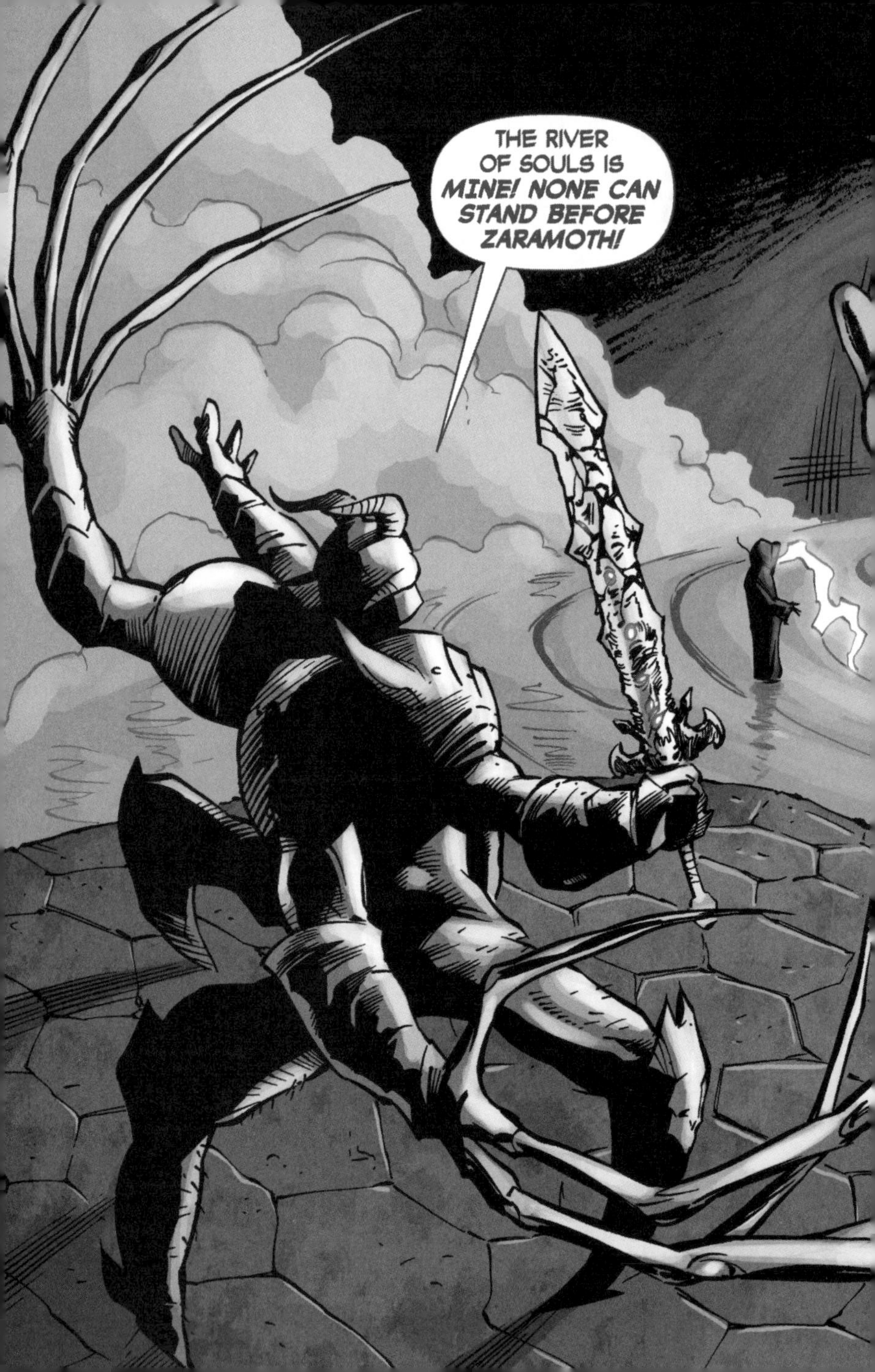
THE RIVER OF SOULS IS *MINE! NONE CAN STAND BEFORE ZARAMOTH!*

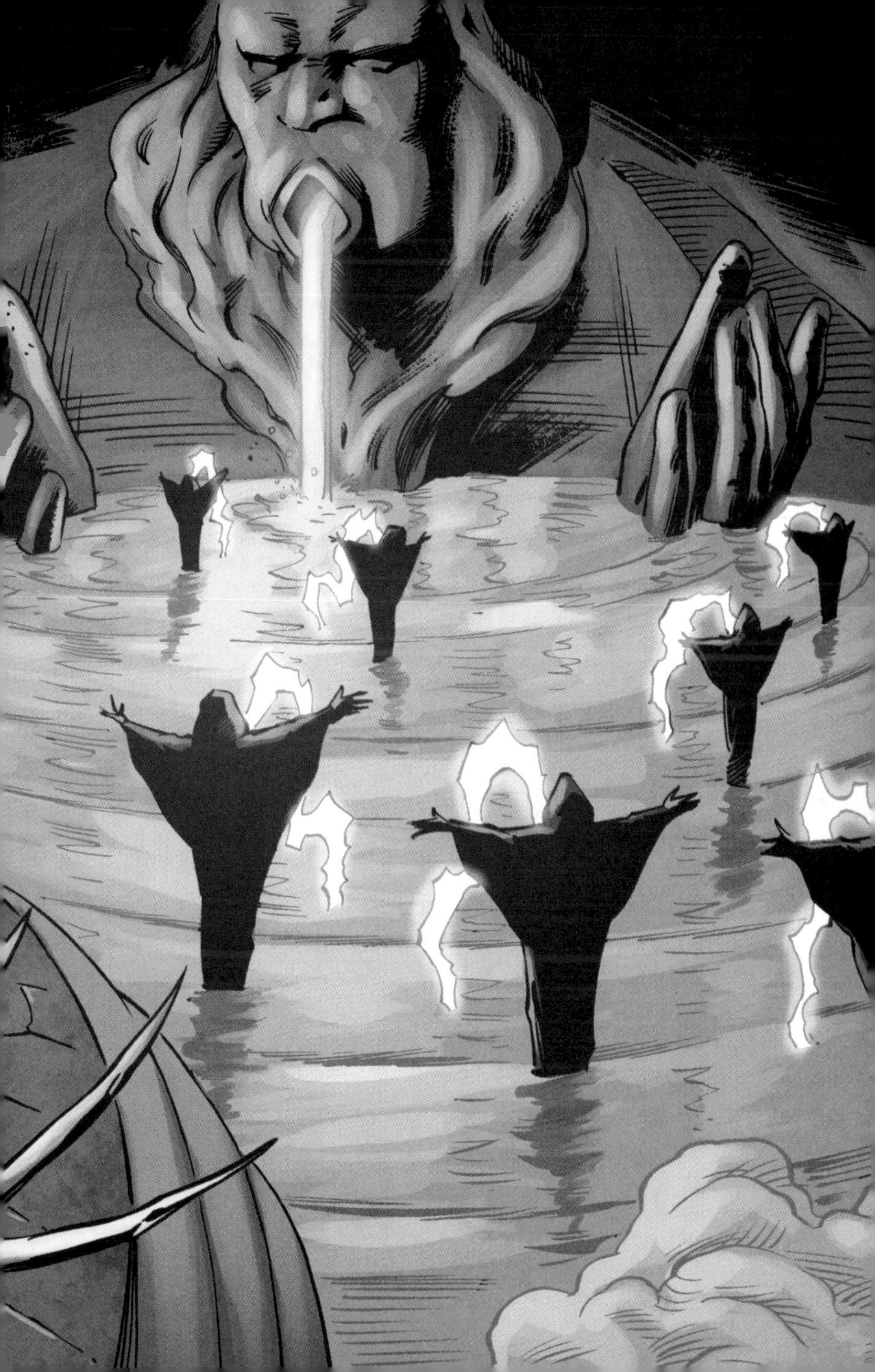

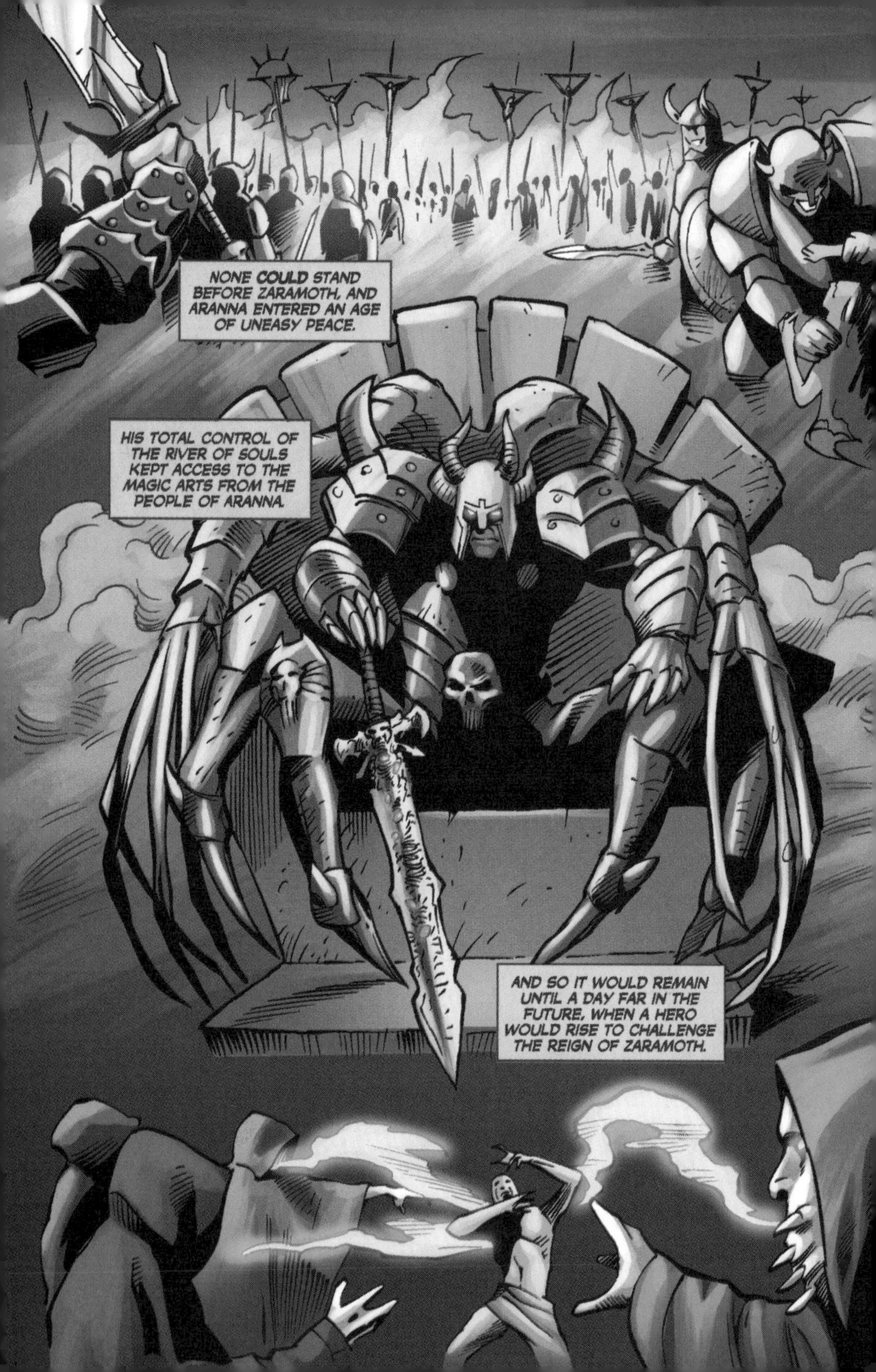
NONE COULD STAND BEFORE ZARAMOTH, AND ARANNA ENTERED AN AGE OF UNEASY PEACE.
HIS TOTAL CONTROL OF THE RIVER OF SOULS KEPT ACCESS TO THE MAGIC ARTS FROM THE PEOPLE OF ARANNA.
AND SO IT WOULD REMAIN UNTIL A DAY FAR IN THE FUTURE, WHEN A HERO WOULD RISE TO CHALLENGE THE REIGN OF ZARAMOTH.

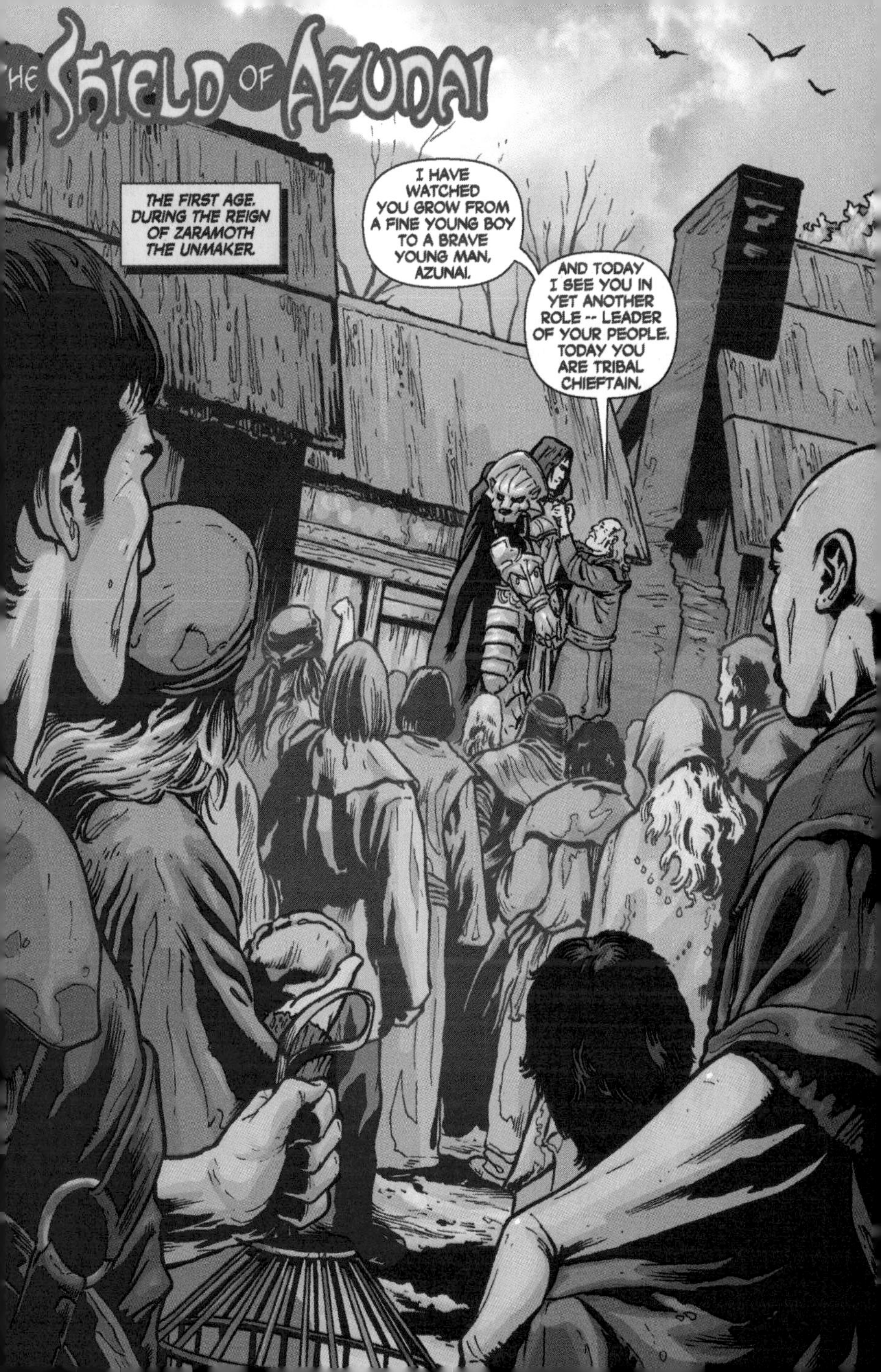

THE SHIELD OF AZUNAI
THE FIRST AGE. DURING THE REIGN OF ZARAMOTH THE UNMAKER.
I HAVE WATCHED YOU GROW FROM A FINE YOUNG BOY TO A BRAVE YOUNG MAN, AZUNAI.
AND TODAY I SEE YOU IN YET ANOTHER ROLE -- LEADER OF YOUR PEOPLE. TODAY YOU ARE TRIBAL CHIEFTAIN.

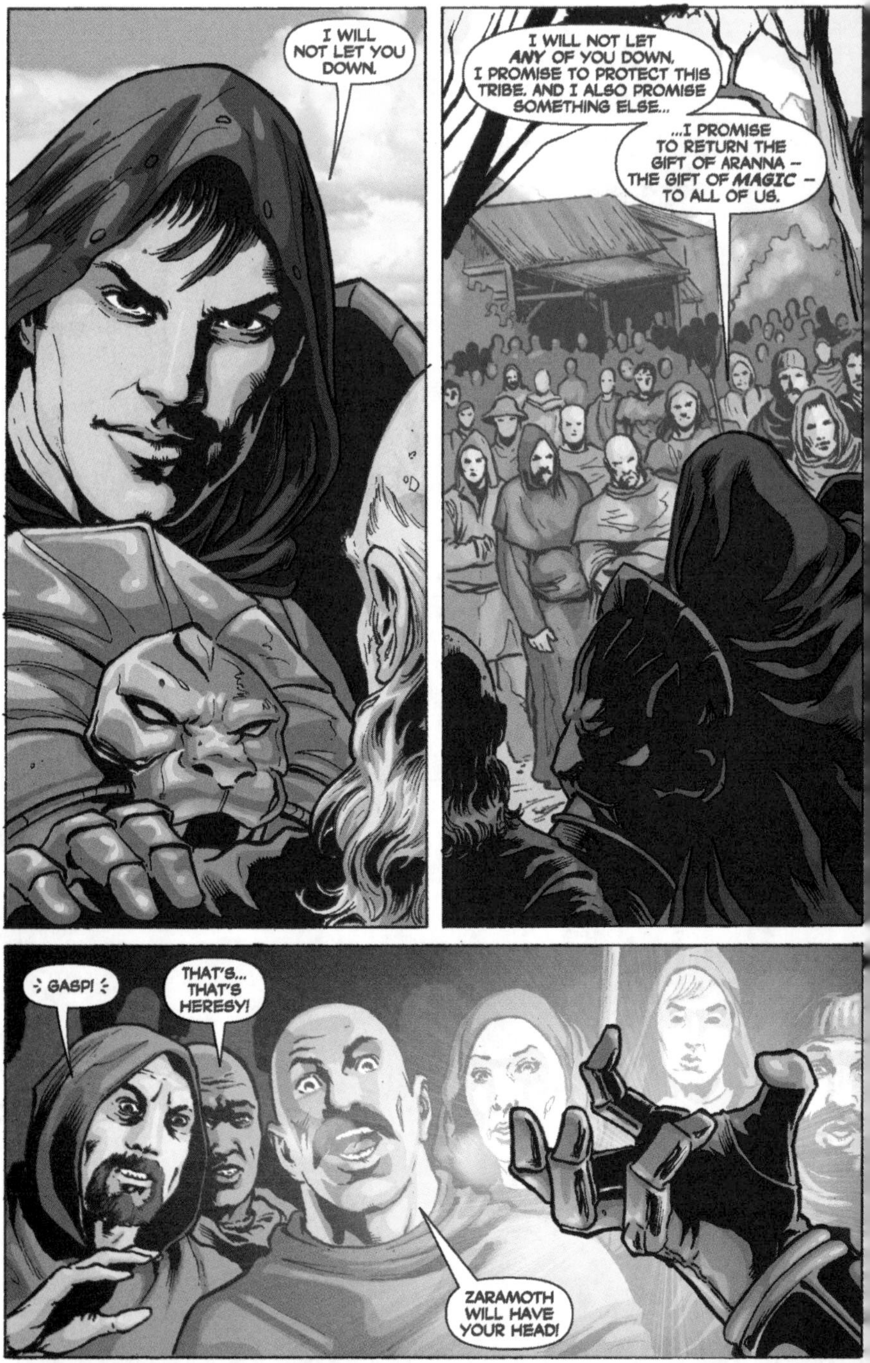
I WILL NOT LET YOU DOWN.
I WILL NOT LET ANY OF YOU DOWN. I PROMISE TO PROTECT THIS TRIBE. AND I ALSO PROMISE SOMETHING ELSE...
...I PROMISE TO RETURN THE GIFT OF ARANNA -- THE GIFT OF MAGIC -- TO ALL OF US.
GASP!
THAT'S... THAT'S HERESY!
ZARAMOTH WILL HAVE YOUR HEAD!

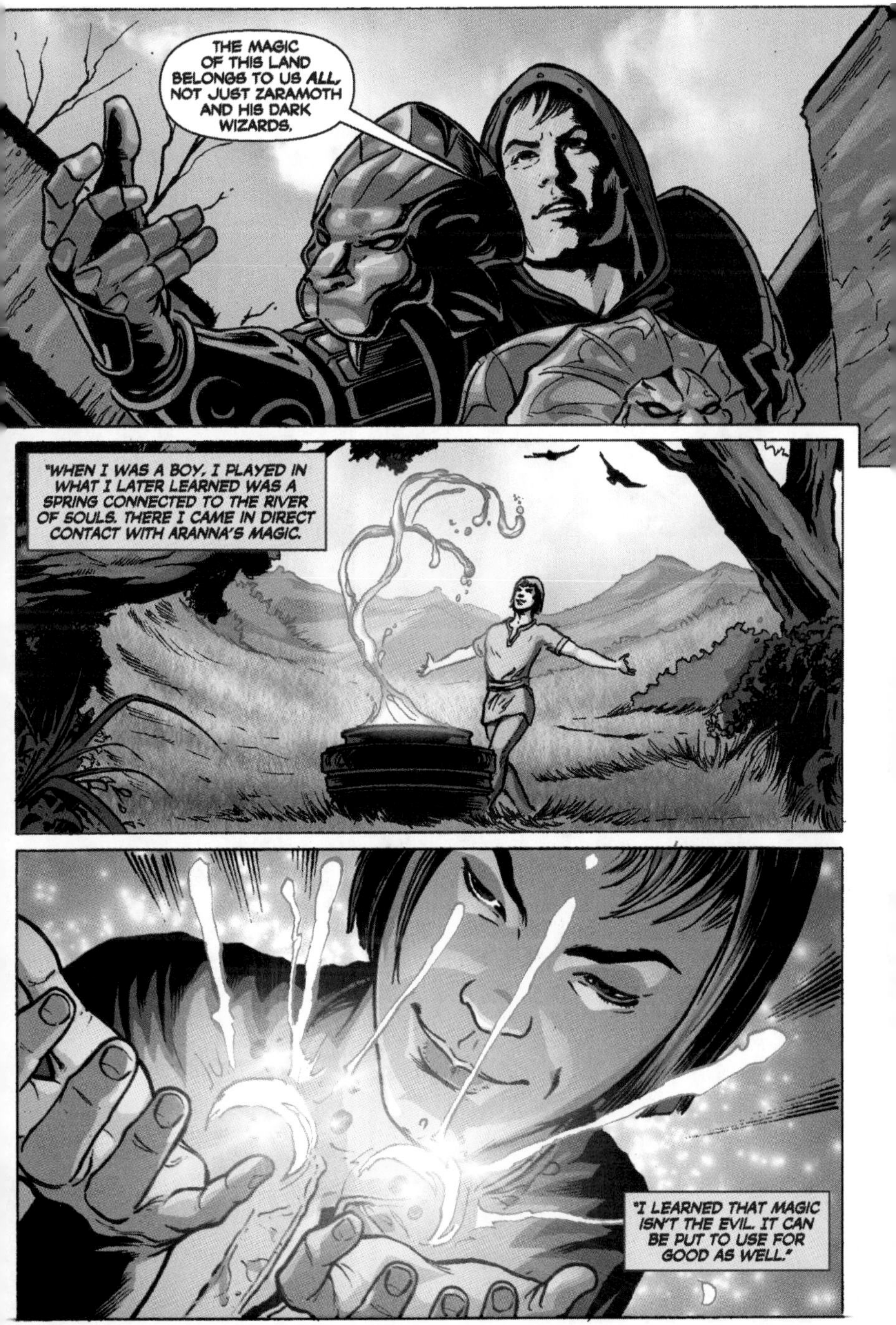
THE MAGIC OF THIS LAND BELONGS TO US ALL, NOT JUST ZARAMOTH AND HIS DARK WIZARDS.
"WHEN I WAS A BOY, I PLAYED IN WHAT I LATER LEARNED WAS A SPRING CONNECTED TO THE RIVER OF SOULS. THERE I CAME IN DIRECT CONTACT WITH ARANNA'S MAGIC.
"I LEARNED THAT MAGIC ISN'T THE EVIL. IT CAN BE PUT TO USE FOR GOOD AS WELL."

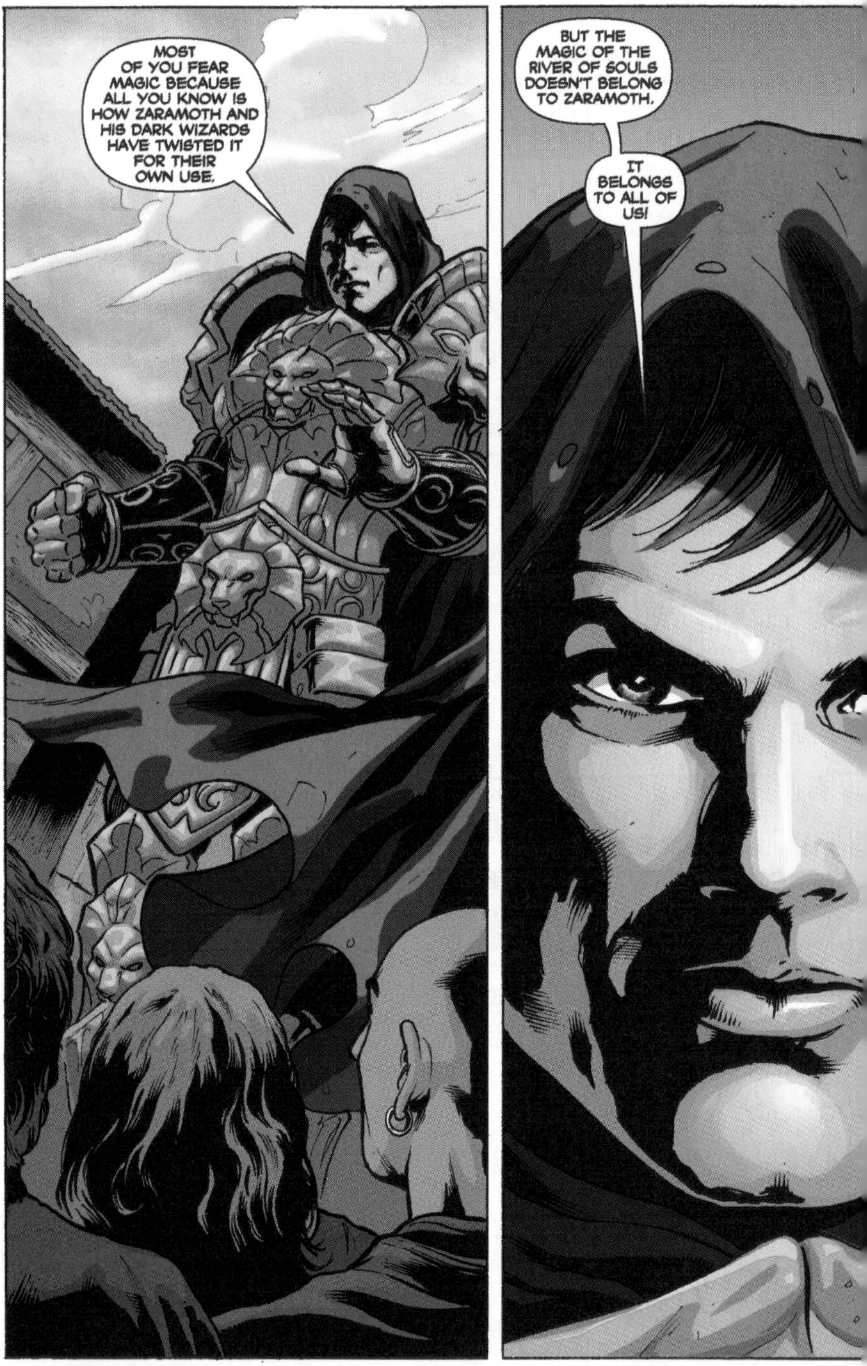
MOST OF YOU FEAR MAGIC BECAUSE ALL YOU KNOW IS HOW ZARAMOTH AND HIS DARK WIZARDS HAVE TWISTED IT FOR THEIR OWN USE.
BUT THE MAGIC OF THE RIVER OF SOULS DOESN'T BELONG TO ZARAMOTH.
IT BELONGS TO ALL OF US!

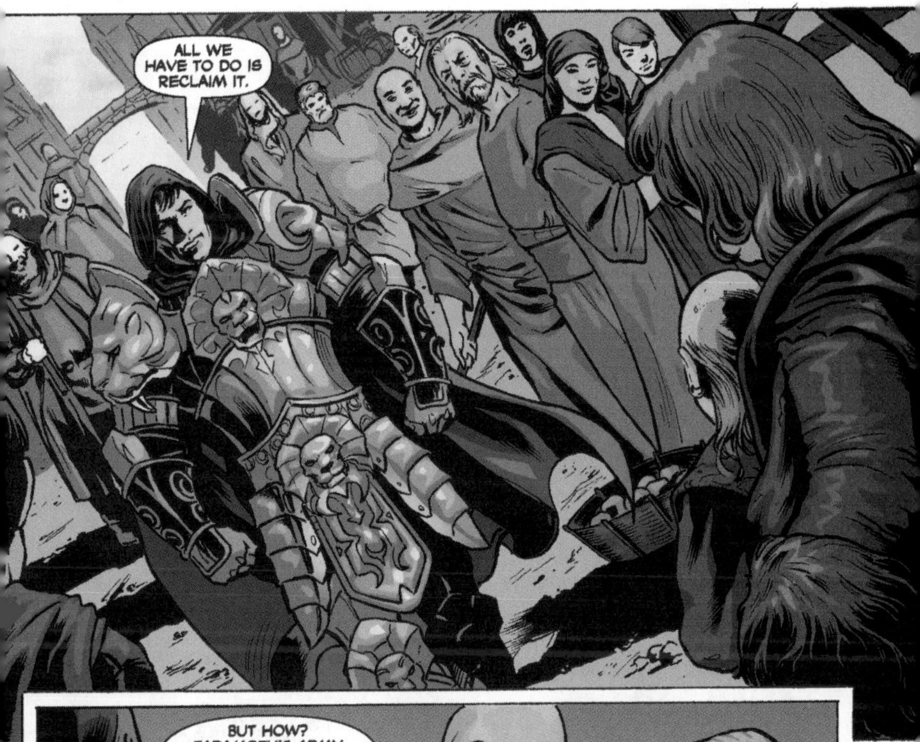
ALL WE HAVE TO DO IS RECLAIM IT.

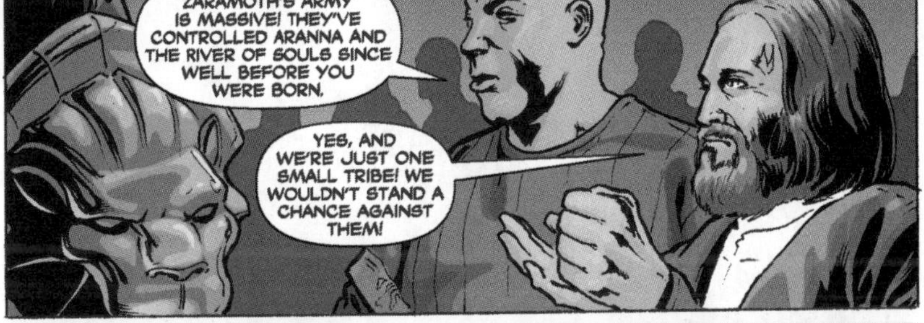
BUT HOW? ZARAMOTH'S ARMY IS MASSIVE! THEY'VE CONTROLLED ARANNA AND THE RIVER OF SOULS SINCE WELL BEFORE YOU WERE BORN.
YES, AND WE'RE JUST ONE SMALL TRIBE! WE WOULDN'T STAND A CHANCE AGAINST THEM!

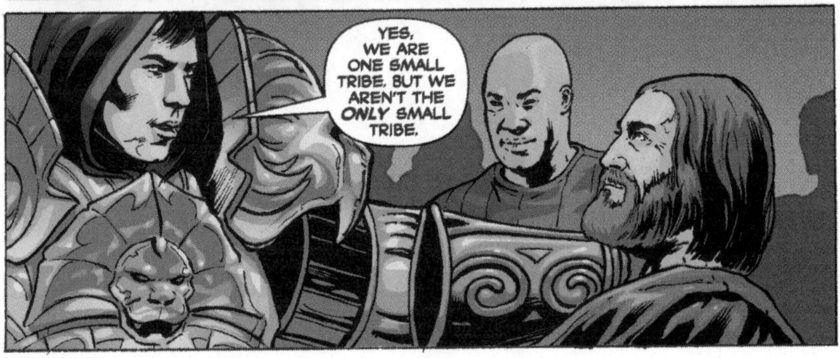
YES, WE ARE ONE SMALL TRIBE. BUT WE AREN'T THE *ONLY* SMALL TRIBE.

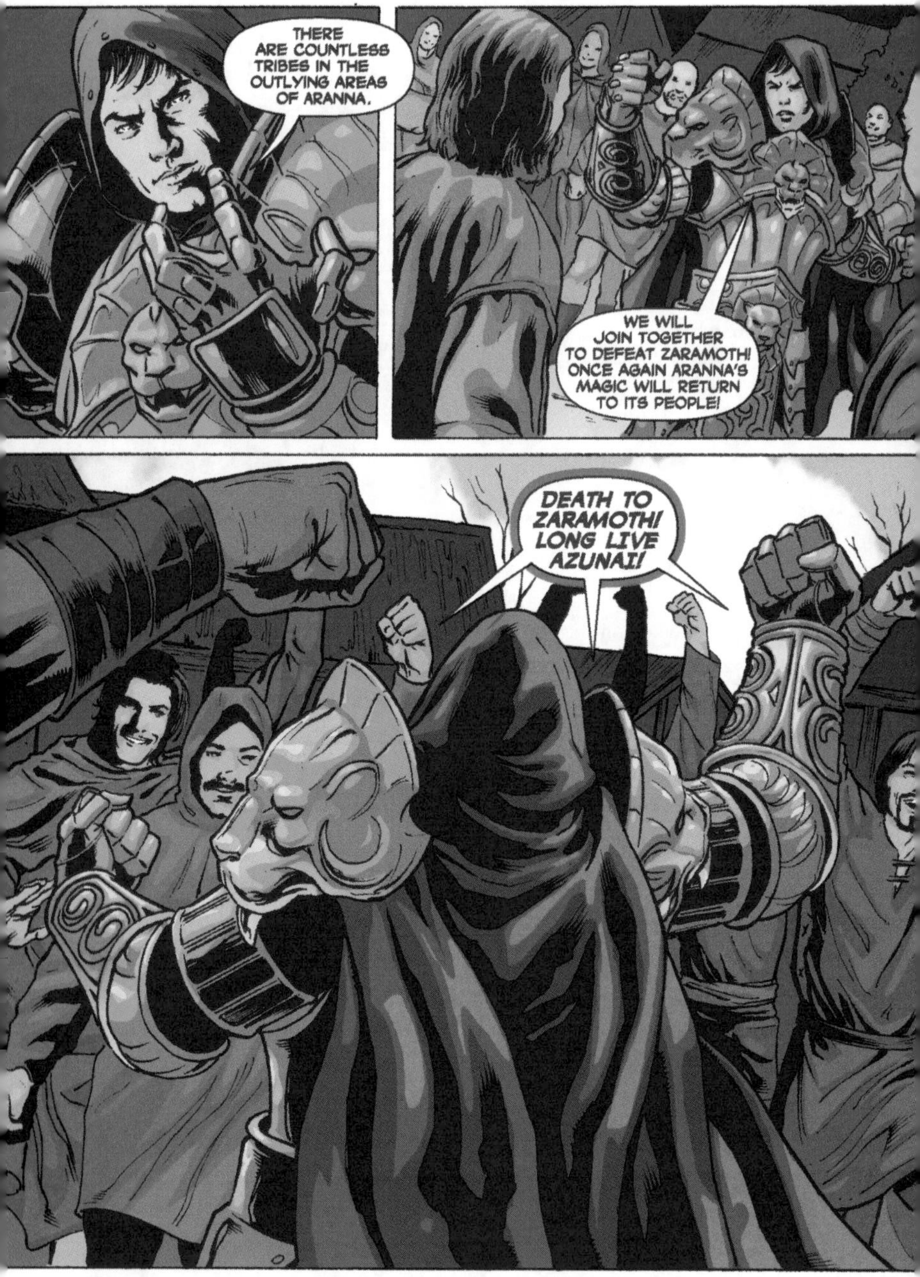
THERE ARE COUNTLESS TRIBES IN THE OUTLYING AREAS OF ARANNA.
WE WILL JOIN TOGETHER TO DEFEAT ZARAMOTH! ONCE AGAIN ARANNA'S MAGIC WILL RETURN TO ITS PEOPLE!
DEATH TO ZARAMOTH! LONG LIVE AZUNAI!

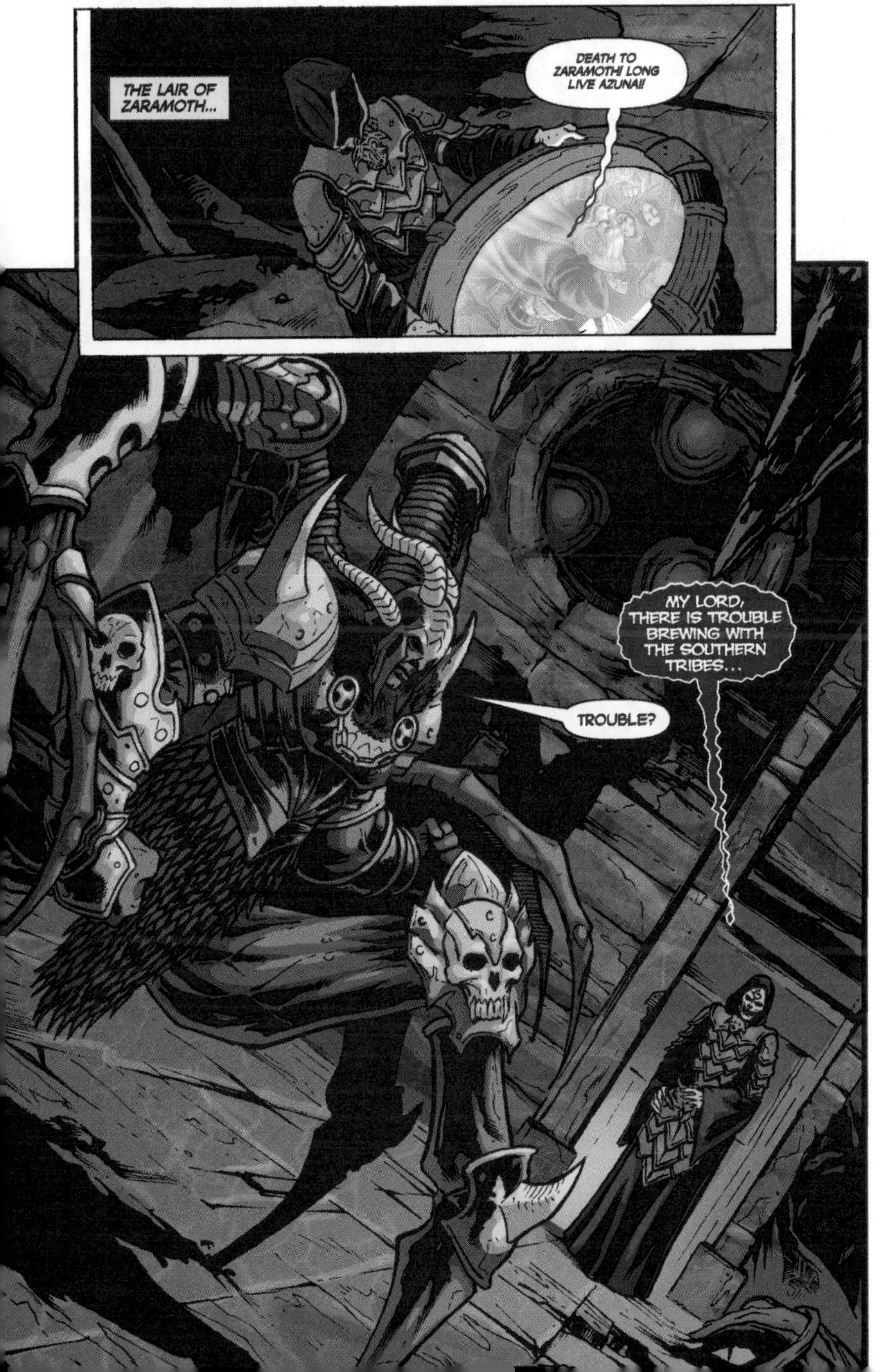

THE LAIR OF ZARAMOTH...
DEATH TO ZARAMOTH! LONG LIVE AZUNAI!
MY LORD, THERE IS TROUBLE BREWING WITH THE SOUTHERN TRIBES...
TROUBLE?

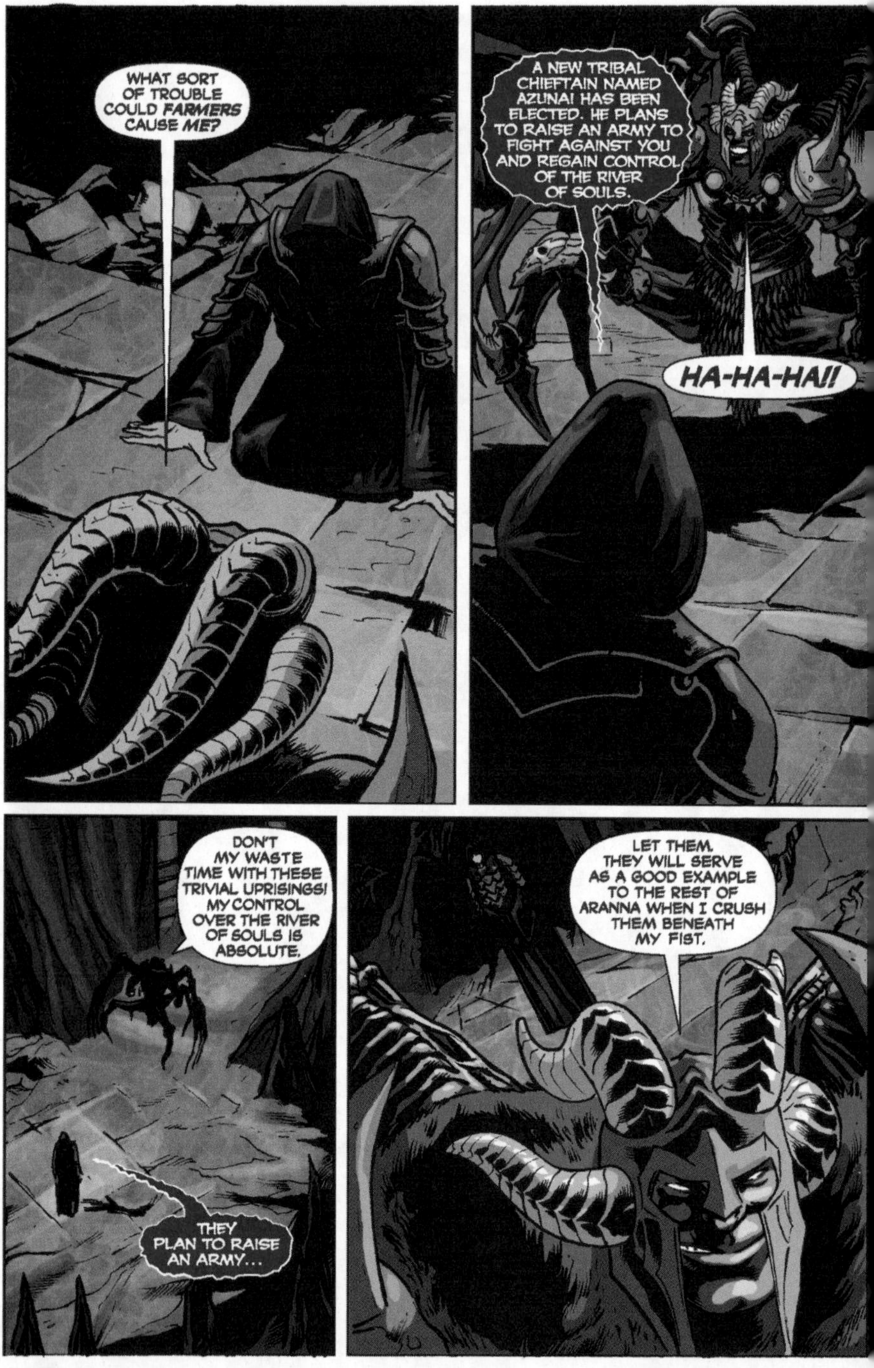
WHAT SORT OF TROUBLE COULD FARMERS CAUSE ME?
A NEW TRIBAL CHIEFTAIN NAMED AZUNAI HAS BEEN ELECTED. HE PLANS TO RAISE AN ARMY TO FIGHT AGAINST YOU AND REGAIN CONTROL OF THE RIVER OF SOULS.
HA-HA-HA!!
DON'T MY WASTE TIME WITH THESE TRIVIAL UPRISINGS! MY CONTROL OVER THE RIVER OF SOULS IS ABSOLUTE.
THEY PLAN TO RAISE AN ARMY...
LET THEM. THEY WILL SERVE AS A GOOD EXAMPLE TO THE REST OF ARANNA WHEN I CRUSH THEM BENEATH MY FIST.

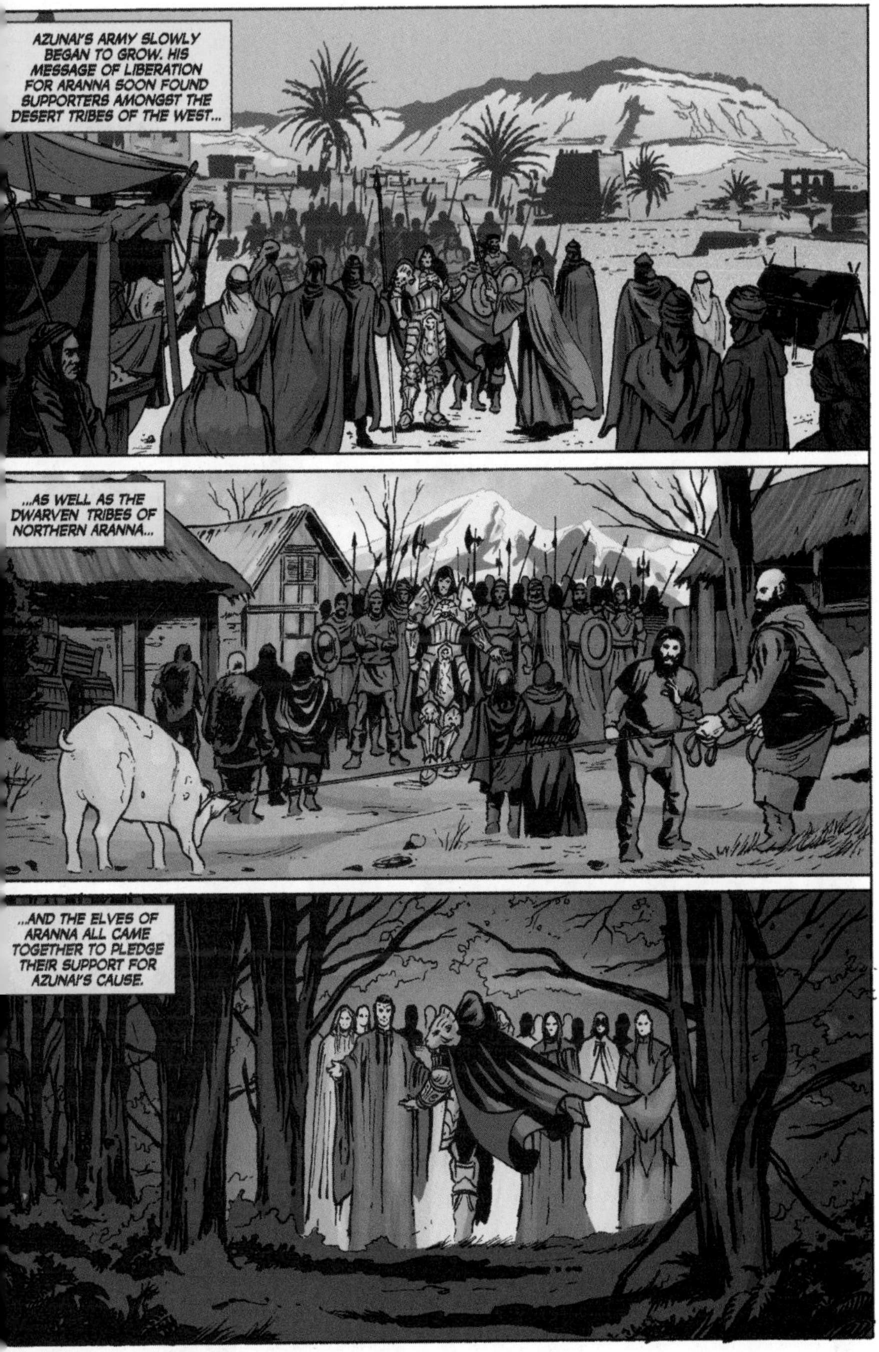
AZUNAI'S ARMY SLOWLY BEGAN TO GROW. HIS MESSAGE OF LIBERATION FOR ARANNA SOON FOUND SUPPORTERS AMONGST THE DESERT TRIBES OF THE WEST...
...AS WELL AS THE DWARVEN TRIBES OF NORTHERN ARANNA...
...AND THE ELVES OF ARANNA ALL CAME TOGETHER TO PLEDGE THEIR SUPPORT FOR AZUNAI'S CAUSE.

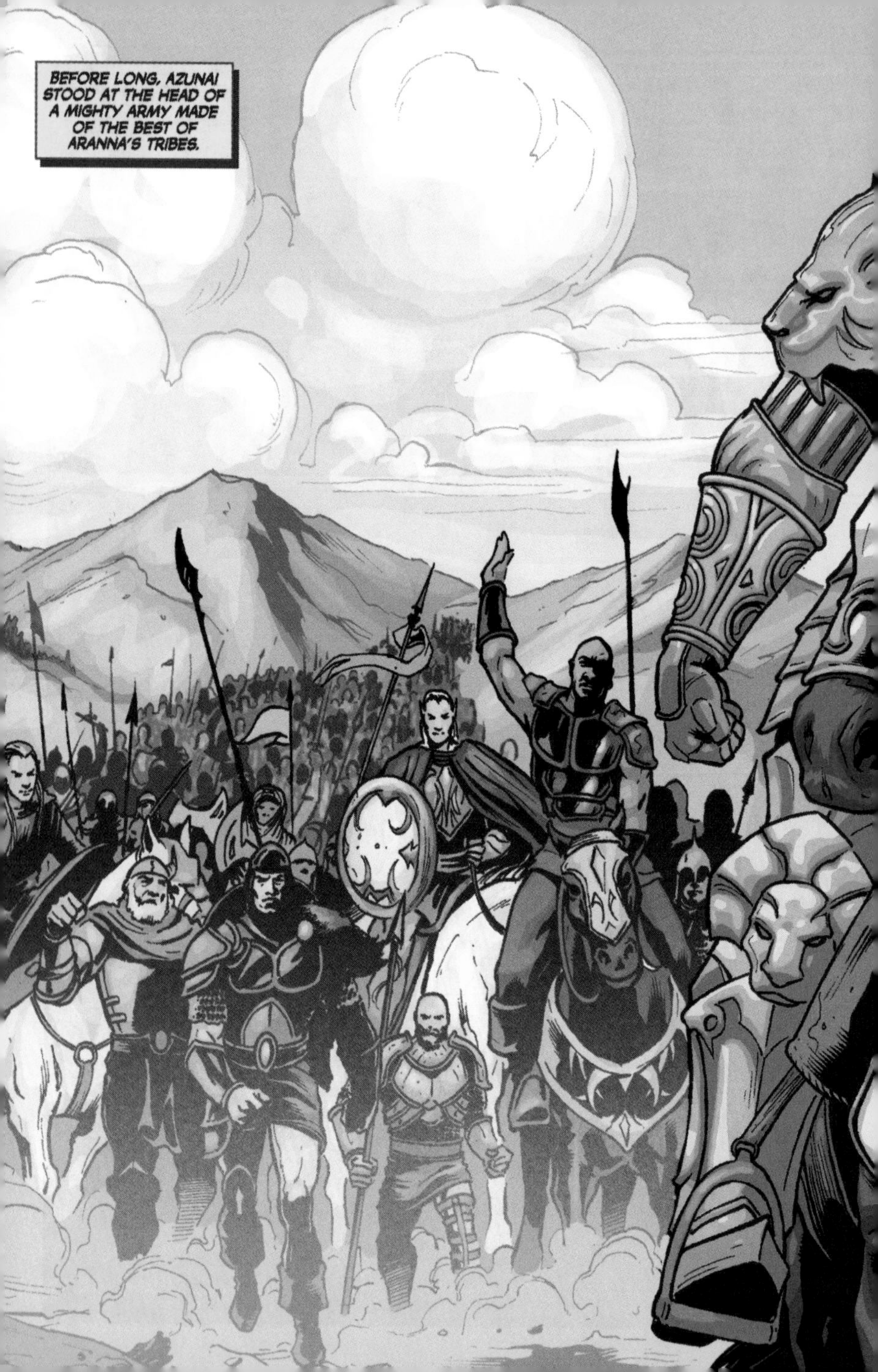
BEFORE LONG, AZUNAI STOOD AT THE HEAD OF A MIGHTY ARMY MADE OF THE BEST OF ARANNA'S TRIBES.

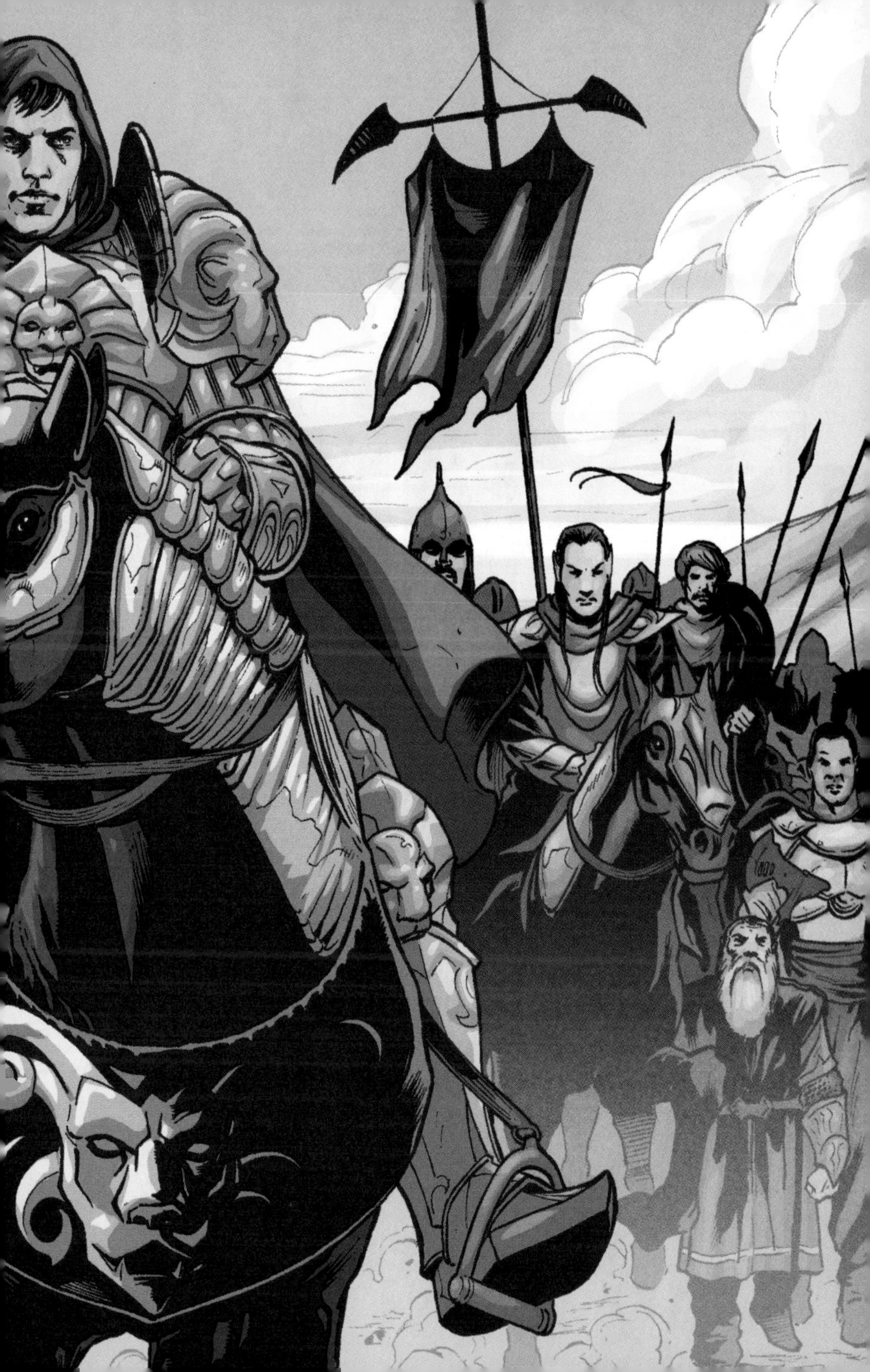

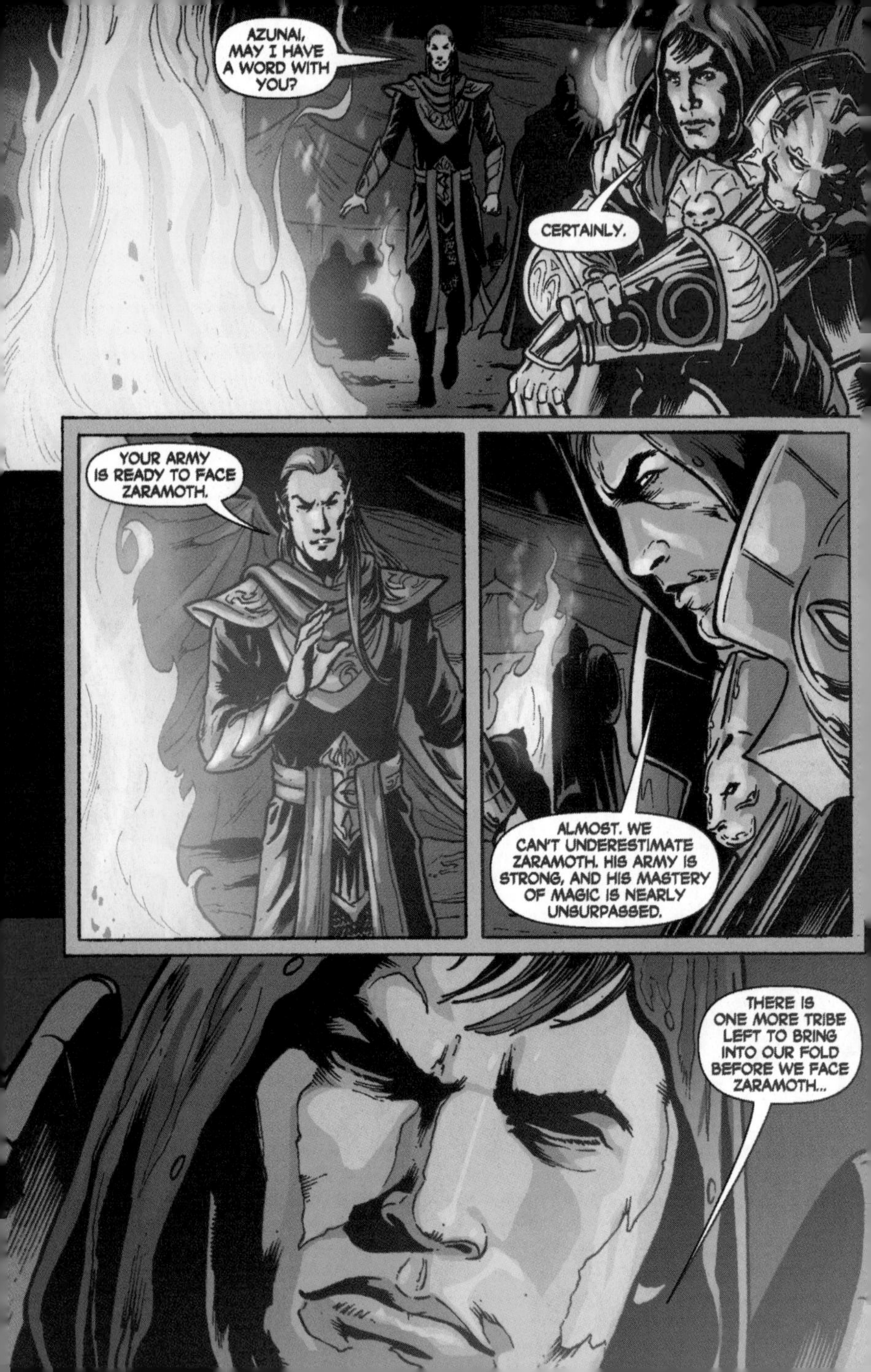
AZUNAI, MAY I HAVE A WORD WITH YOU?
CERTAINLY.
YOUR ARMY IS READY TO FACE ZARAMOTH.
ALMOST. WE CAN'T UNDERESTIMATE ZARAMOTH. HIS ARMY IS STRONG, AND HIS MASTERY OF MAGIC IS NEARLY UNSURPASSED.
THERE IS ONE MORE TRIBE LEFT TO BRING INTO OUR FOLD BEFORE WE FACE ZARAMOTH...

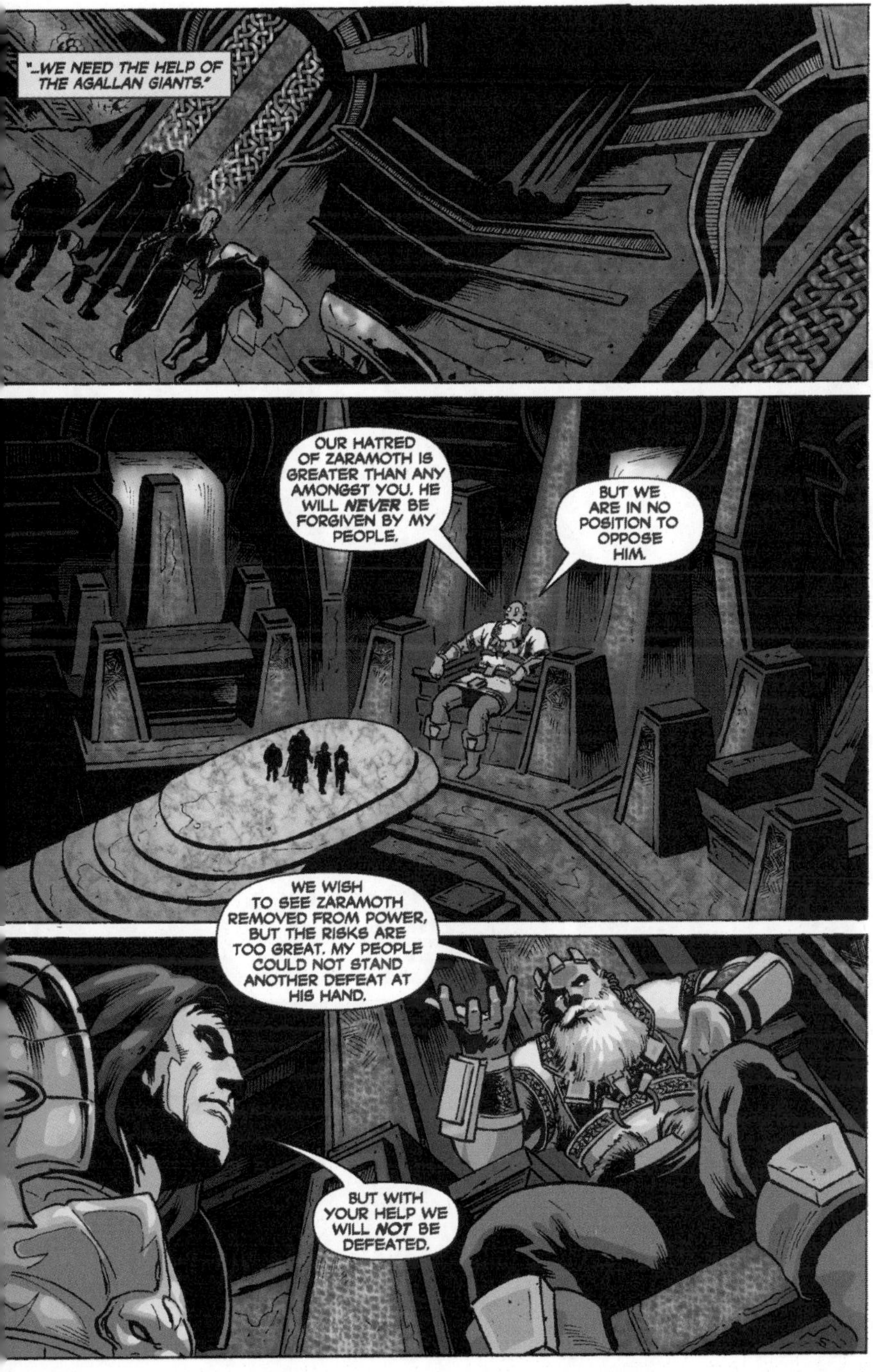
"...WE NEED THE HELP OF THE AGALLAN GIANTS."
OUR HATRED OF ZARAMOTH IS GREATER THAN ANY AMONGST YOU. HE WILL *NEVER* BE FORGIVEN BY MY PEOPLE.
BUT WE ARE IN NO POSITION TO OPPOSE HIM.
WE WISH TO SEE ZARAMOTH REMOVED FROM POWER, BUT THE RISKS ARE TOO GREAT. MY PEOPLE COULD NOT STAND ANOTHER DEFEAT AT HIS HAND.
BUT WITH YOUR HELP WE WILL *NOT* BE DEFEATED.

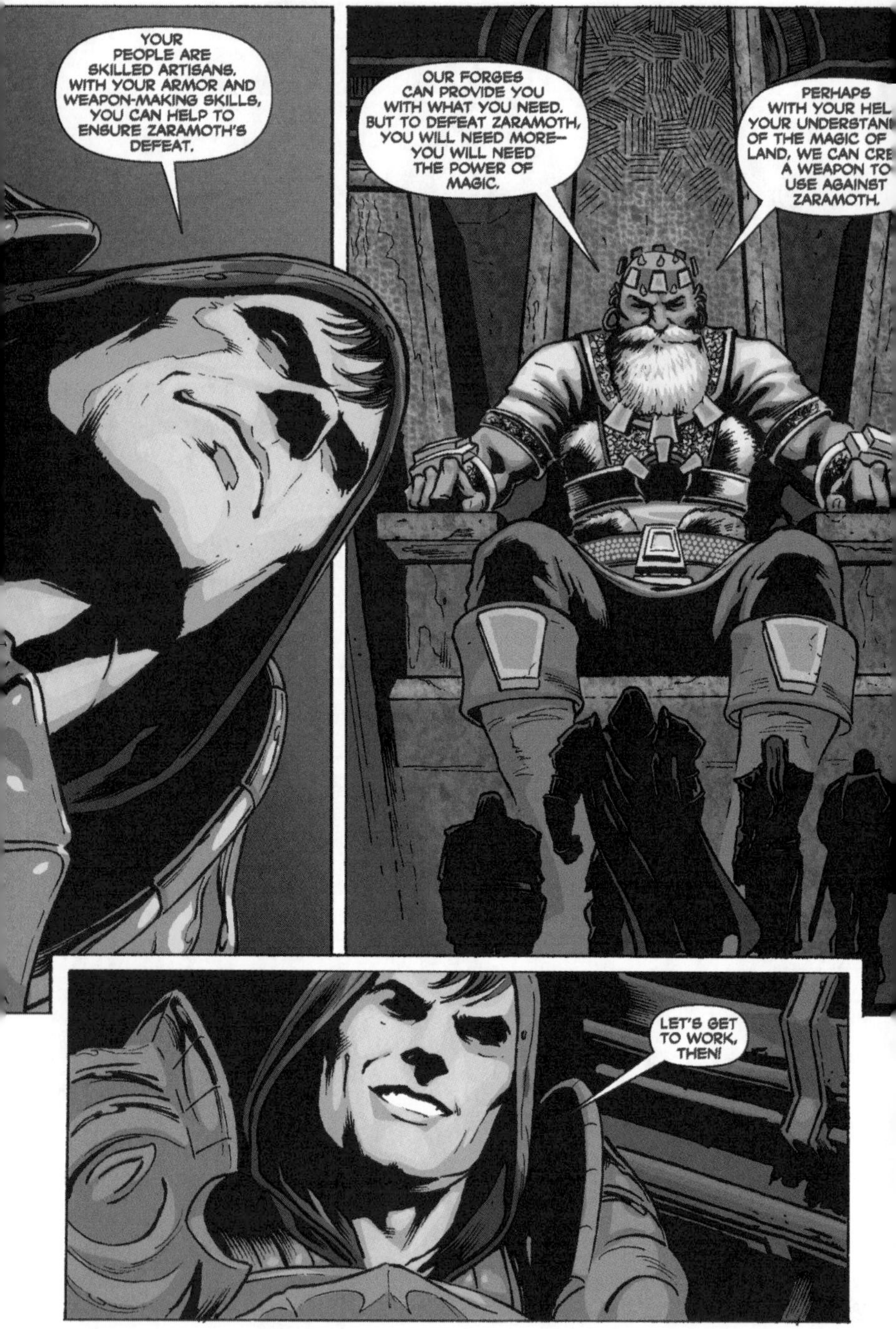
YOUR PEOPLE ARE SKILLED ARTISANS. WITH YOUR ARMOR AND WEAPON-MAKING SKILLS, YOU CAN HELP TO ENSURE ZARAMOTH'S DEFEAT.
OUR FORGES CAN PROVIDE YOU WITH WHAT YOU NEED. BUT TO DEFEAT ZARAMOTH, YOU WILL NEED MORE-- YOU WILL NEED THE POWER OF MAGIC.
PERHAPS WITH YOUR HEL YOUR UNDERSTAN OF THE MAGIC OF LAND, WE CAN CRE A WEAPON TO USE AGAINST ZARAMOTH.
LET'S GET TO WORK, THEN!

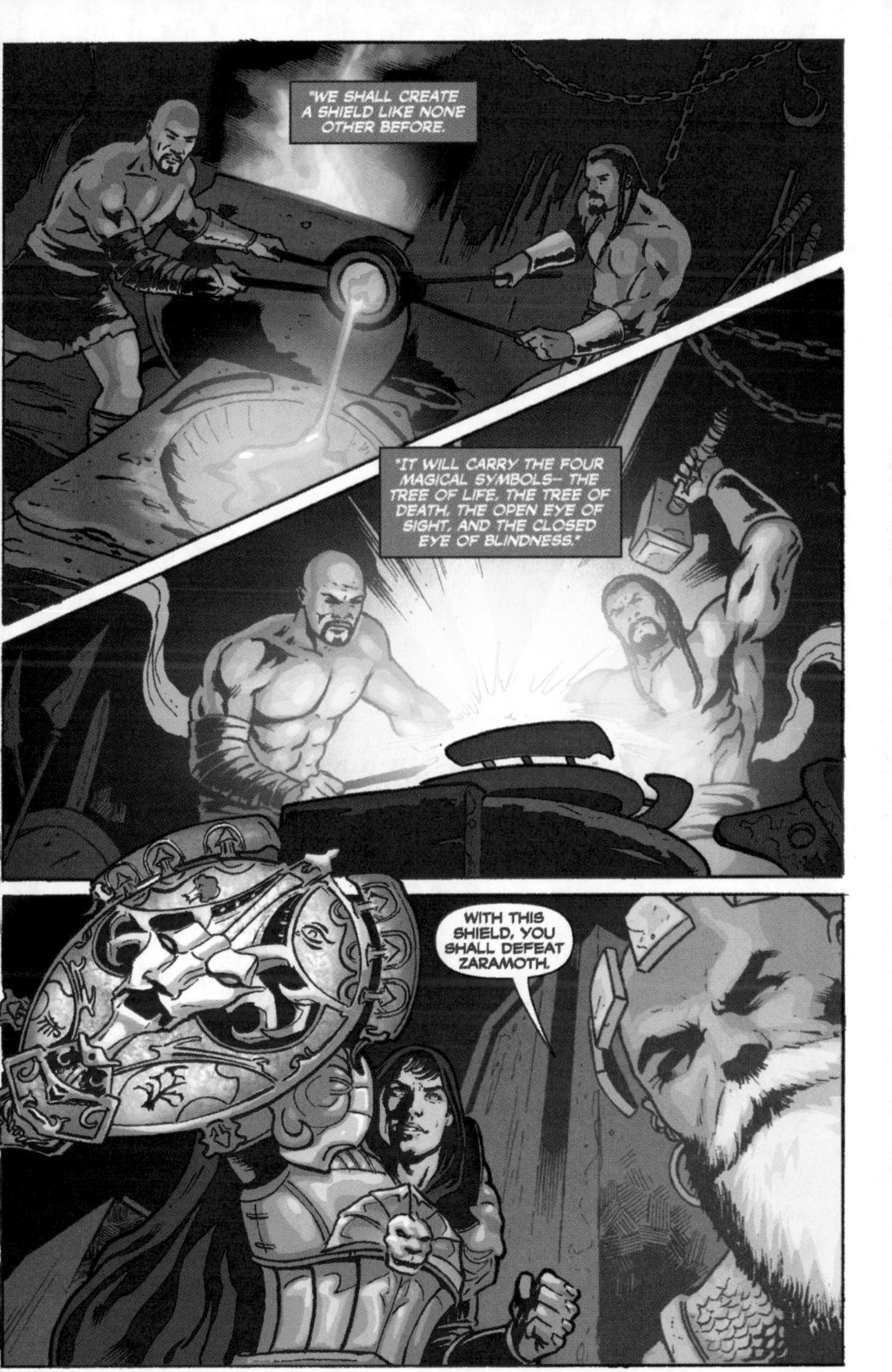
"WE SHALL CREATE A SHIELD LIKE NONE OTHER BEFORE.
"IT WILL CARRY THE FOUR MAGICAL SYMBOLS-- THE TREE OF LIFE, THE TREE OF DEATH, THE OPEN EYE OF SIGHT, AND THE CLOSED EYE OF BLINDNESS."
WITH THIS SHIELD, YOU SHALL DEFEAT ZARAMOTH.

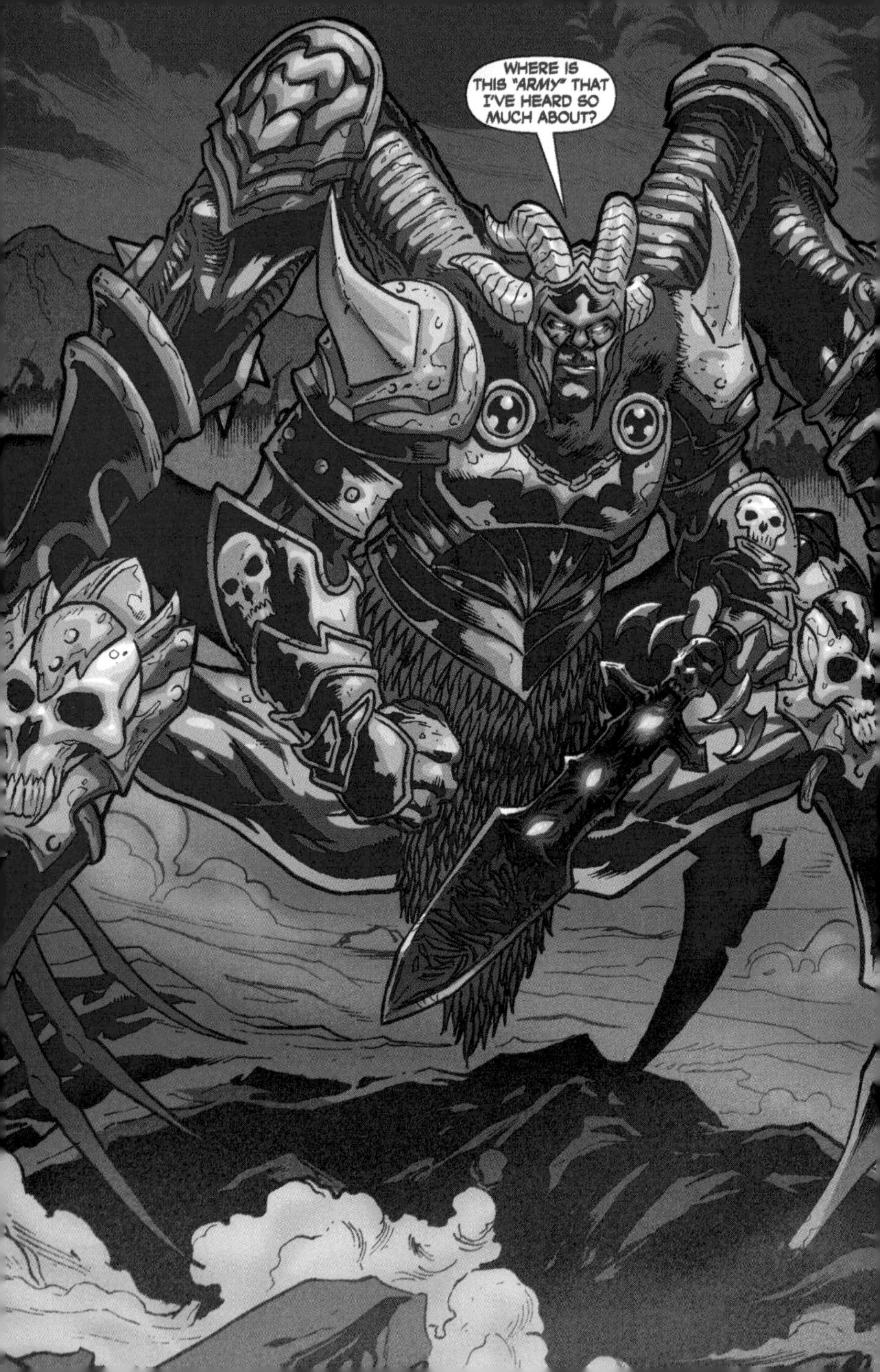
WHERE IS THIS "ARMY" THAT I'VE HEARD SO MUCH ABOUT?

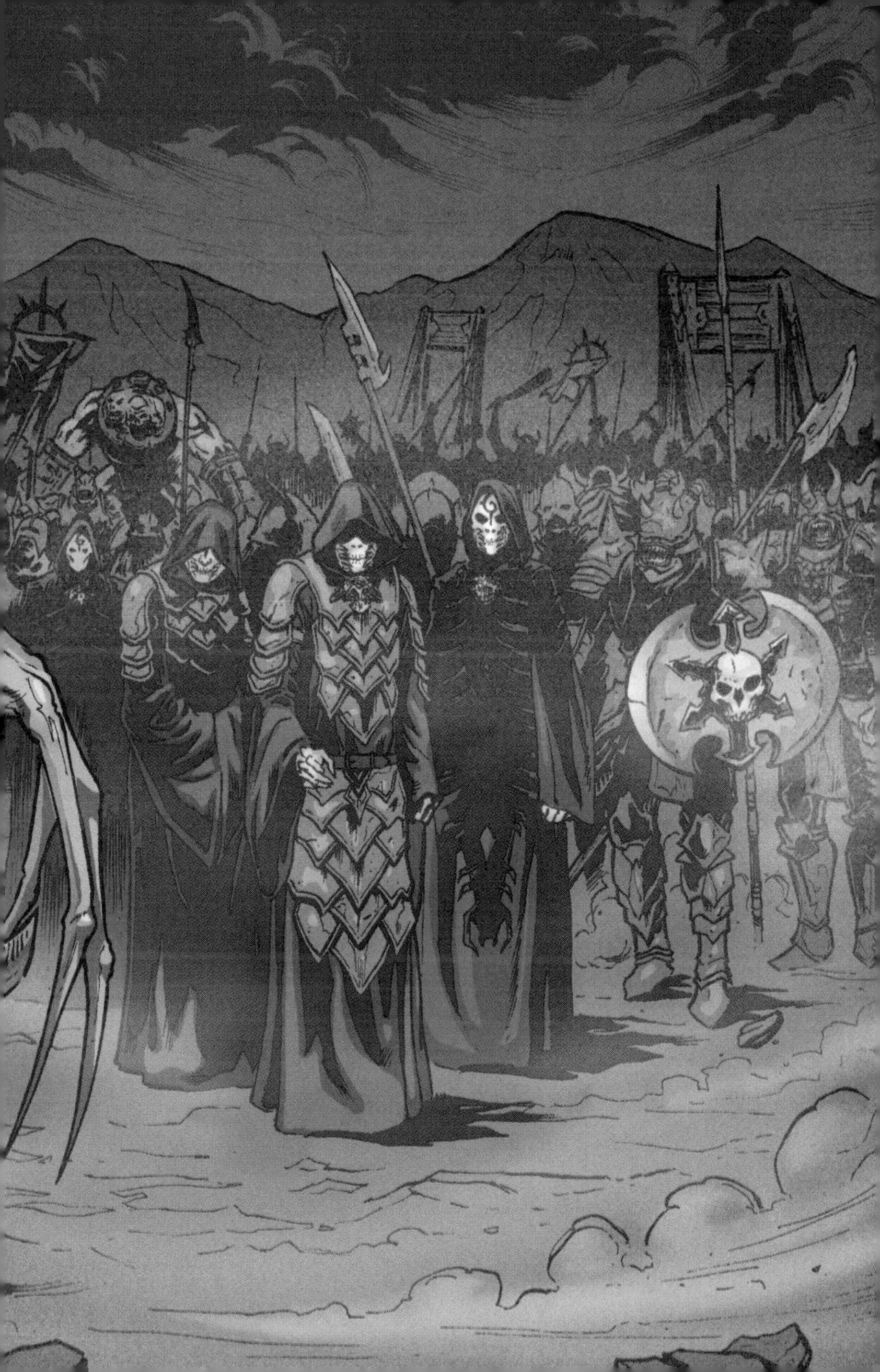

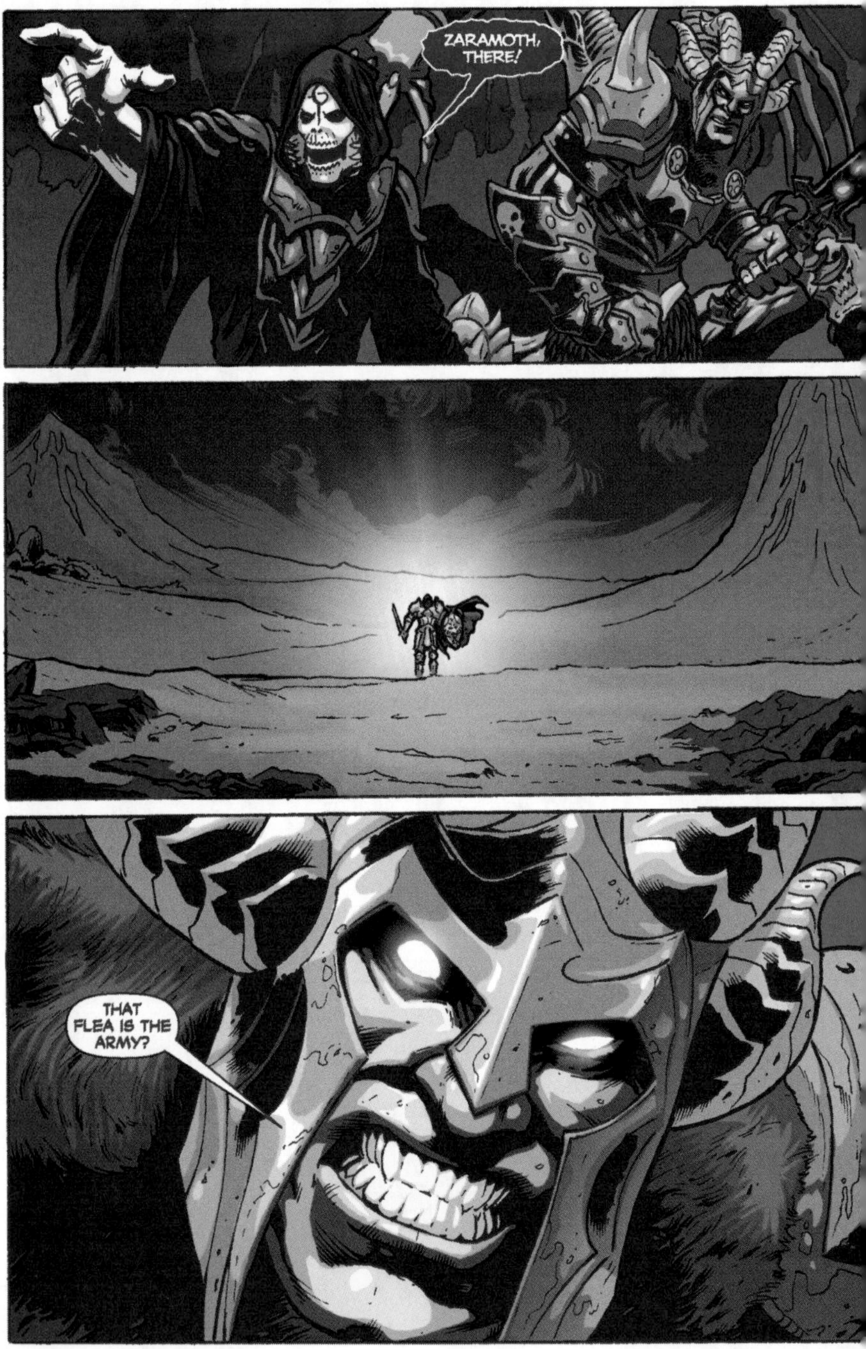
ZARAMOTH, THERE!
THAT FLEA IS THE ARMY?

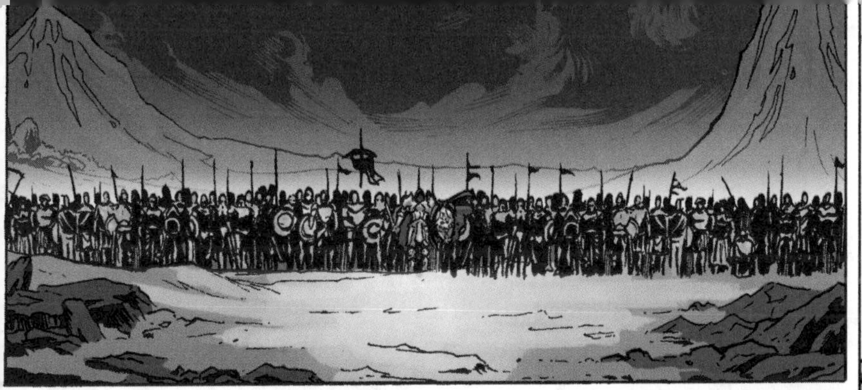

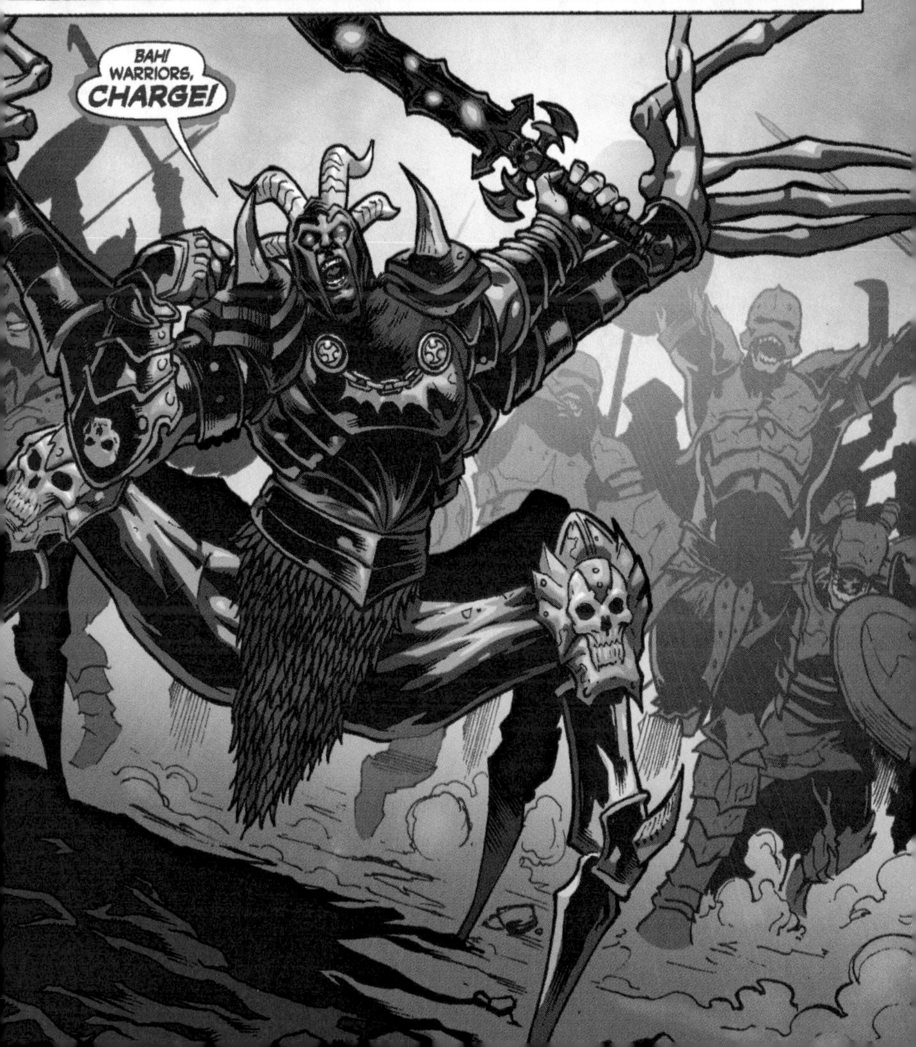
BAH! WARRIORS, CHARGE!

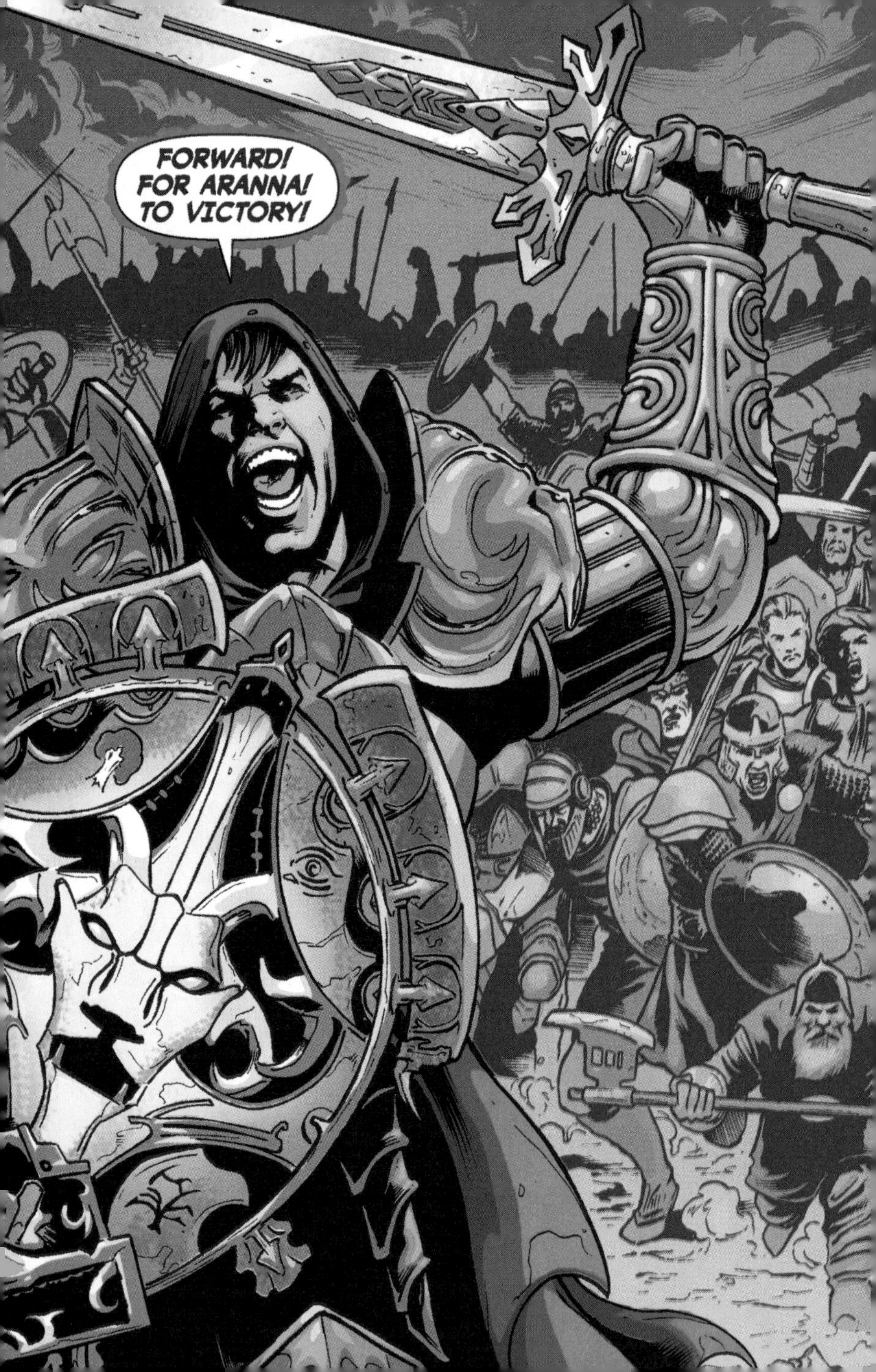
FORWARD! FOR ARANNA! TO VICTORY!

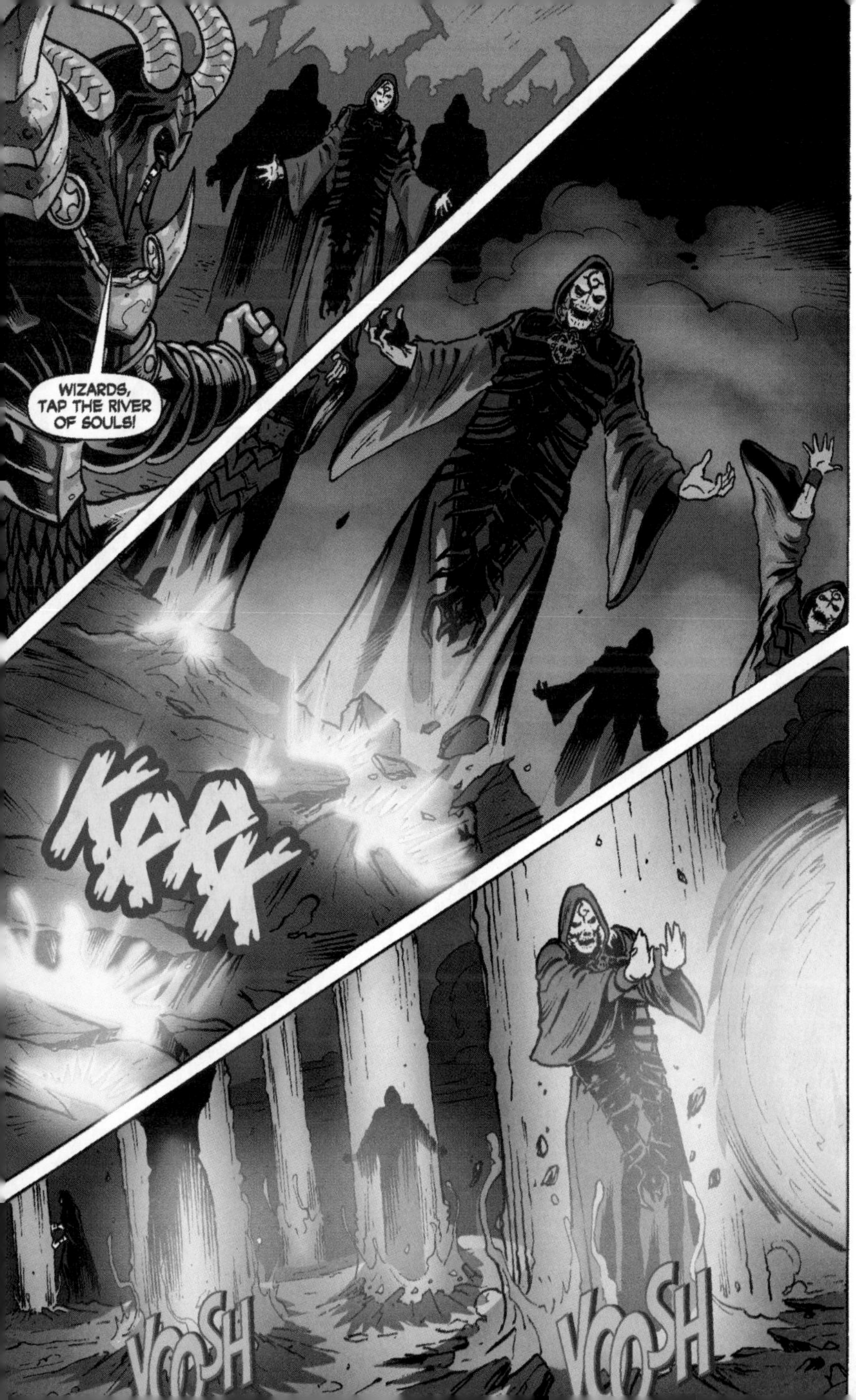
WIZARDS, TAP THE RIVER OF SOULS!
KRAK
VOOSH
VOOSH

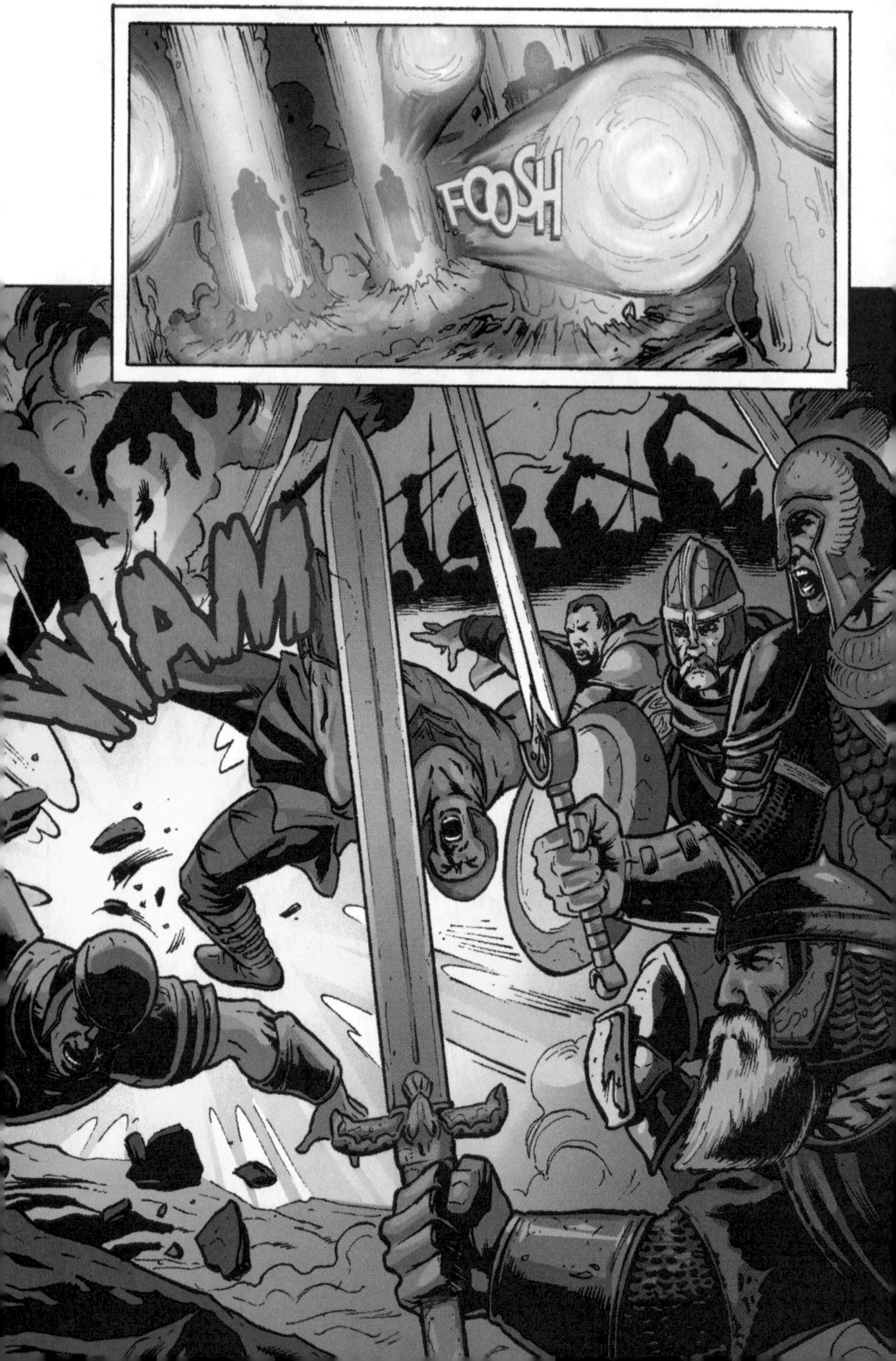
FOOSH
WAM

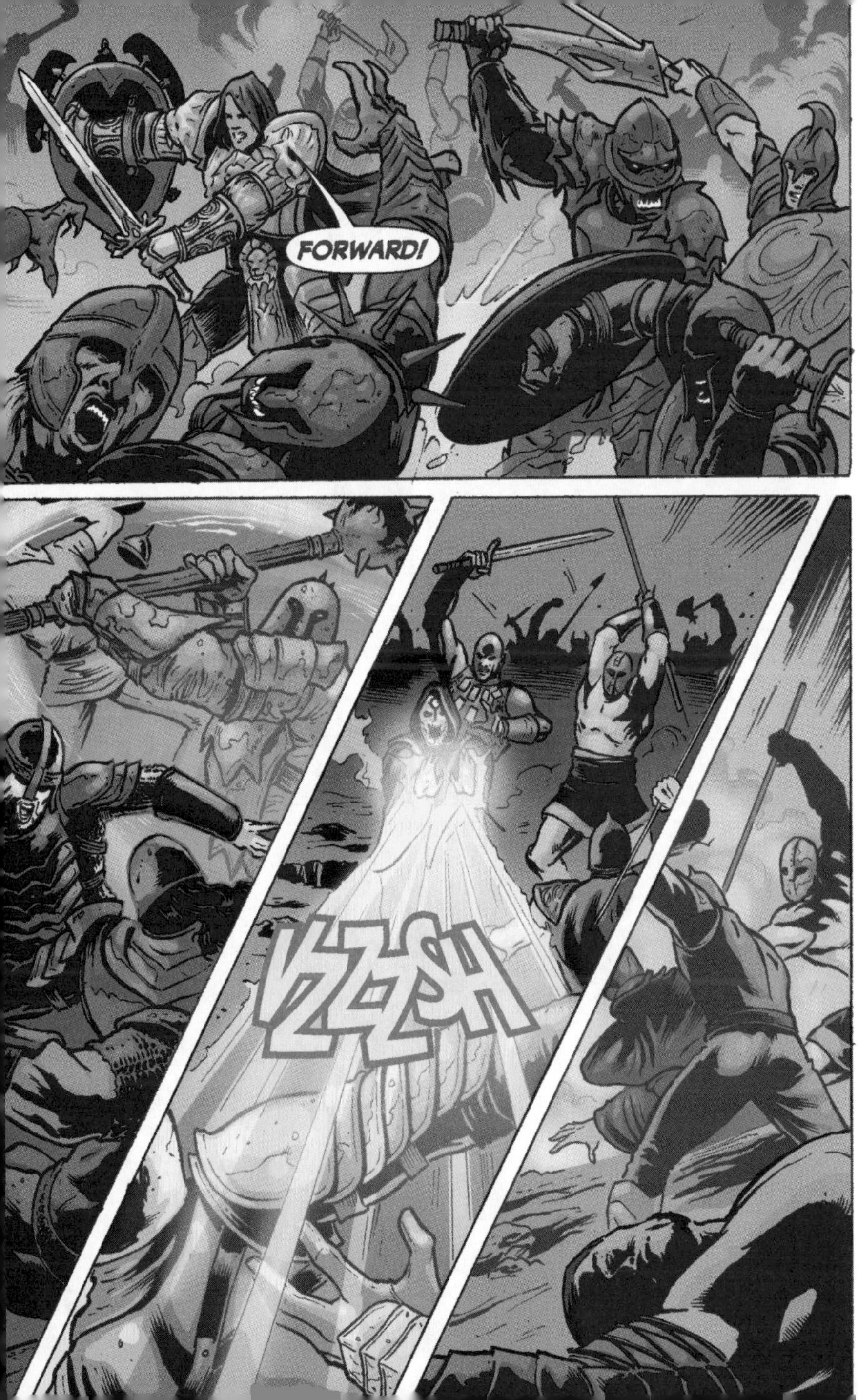
FORWARD!
VZZSH

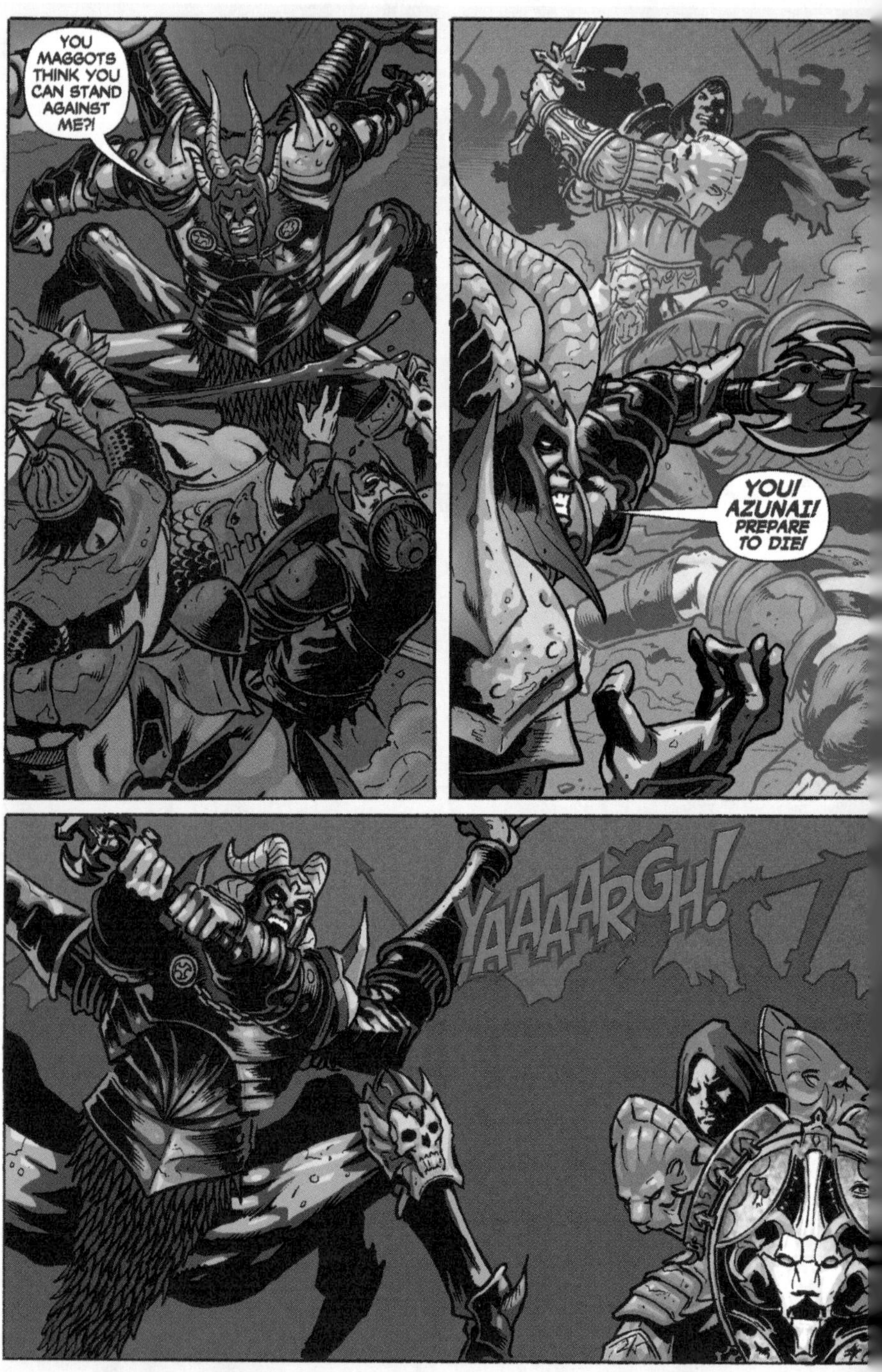
YOU MAGGOTS THINK YOU CAN STAND AGAINST ME?!
YOU! AZUNAI! PREPARE TO DIE!
YAAAARGH!

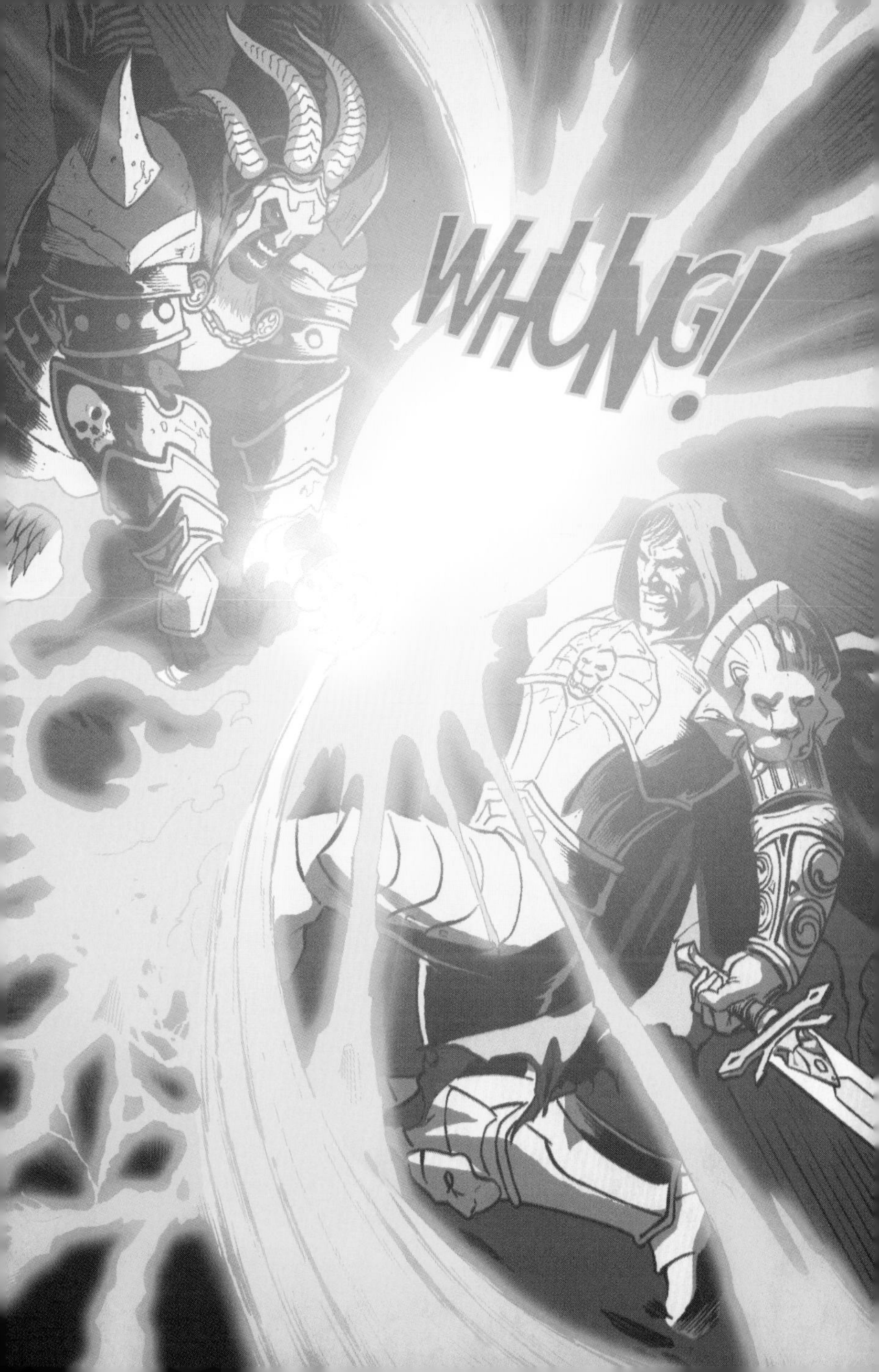
WHUNG!

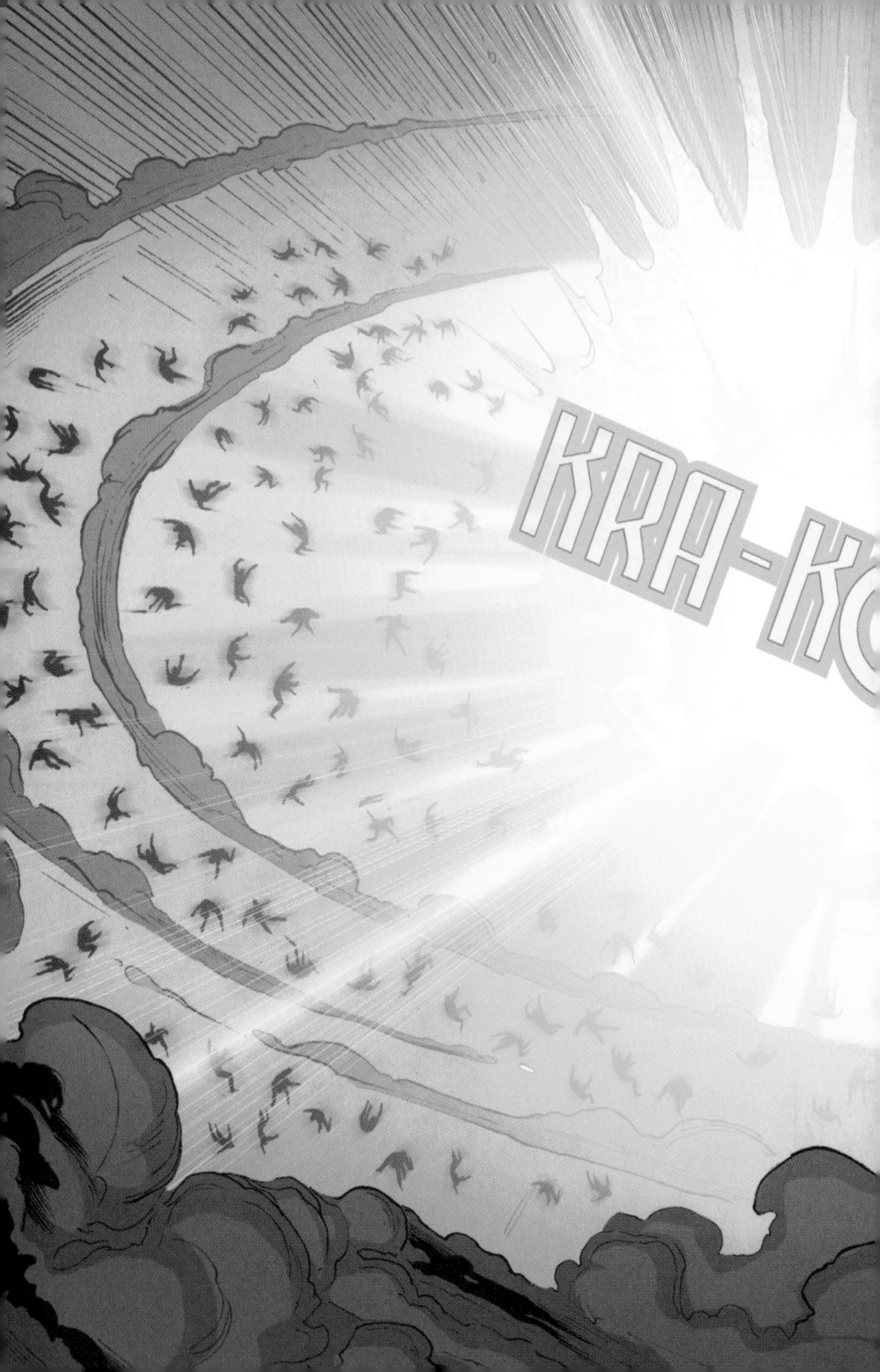
KRA-KO

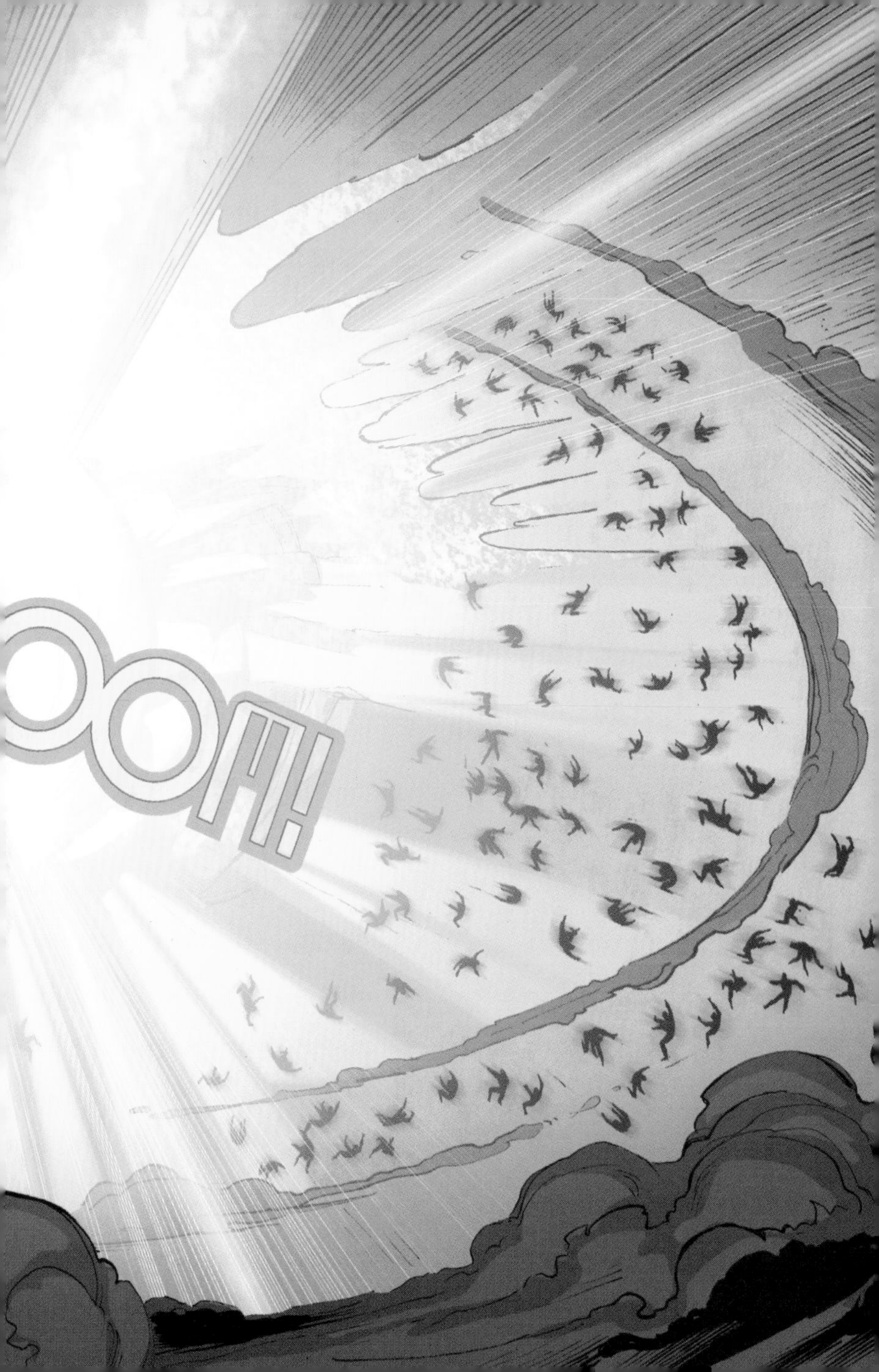
OOM!

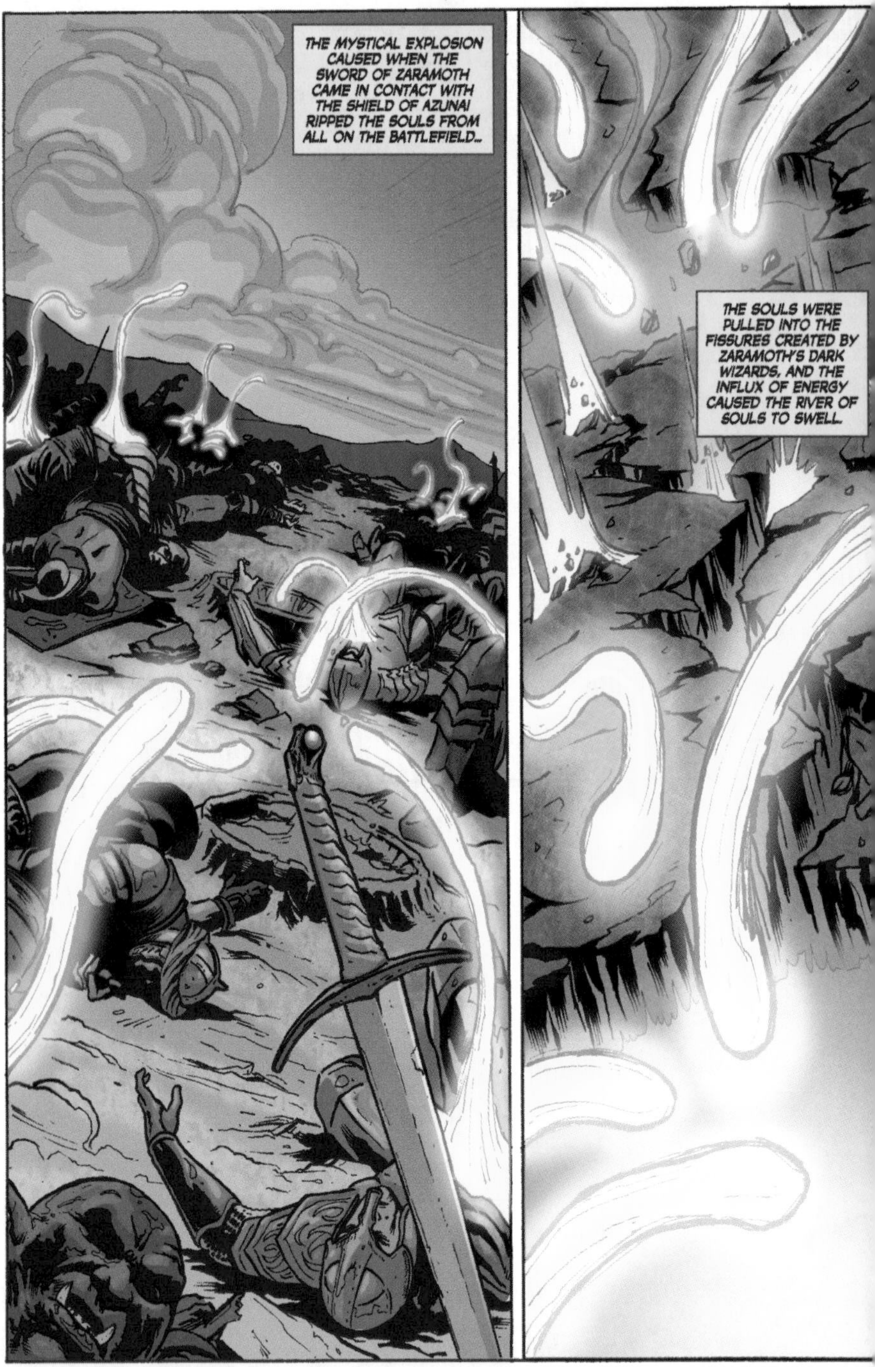
THE MYSTICAL EXPLOSION CAUSED WHEN THE SWORD OF ZARAMOTH CAME IN CONTACT WITH THE SHIELD OF AZUNAI RIPPED THE SOULS FROM ALL ON THE BATTLEFIELD...
THE SOULS WERE PULLED INTO THE FISSURES CREATED BY ZARAMOTH'S DARK WIZARDS, AND THE INFLUX OF ENERGY CAUSED THE RIVER OF SOULS TO SWELL.

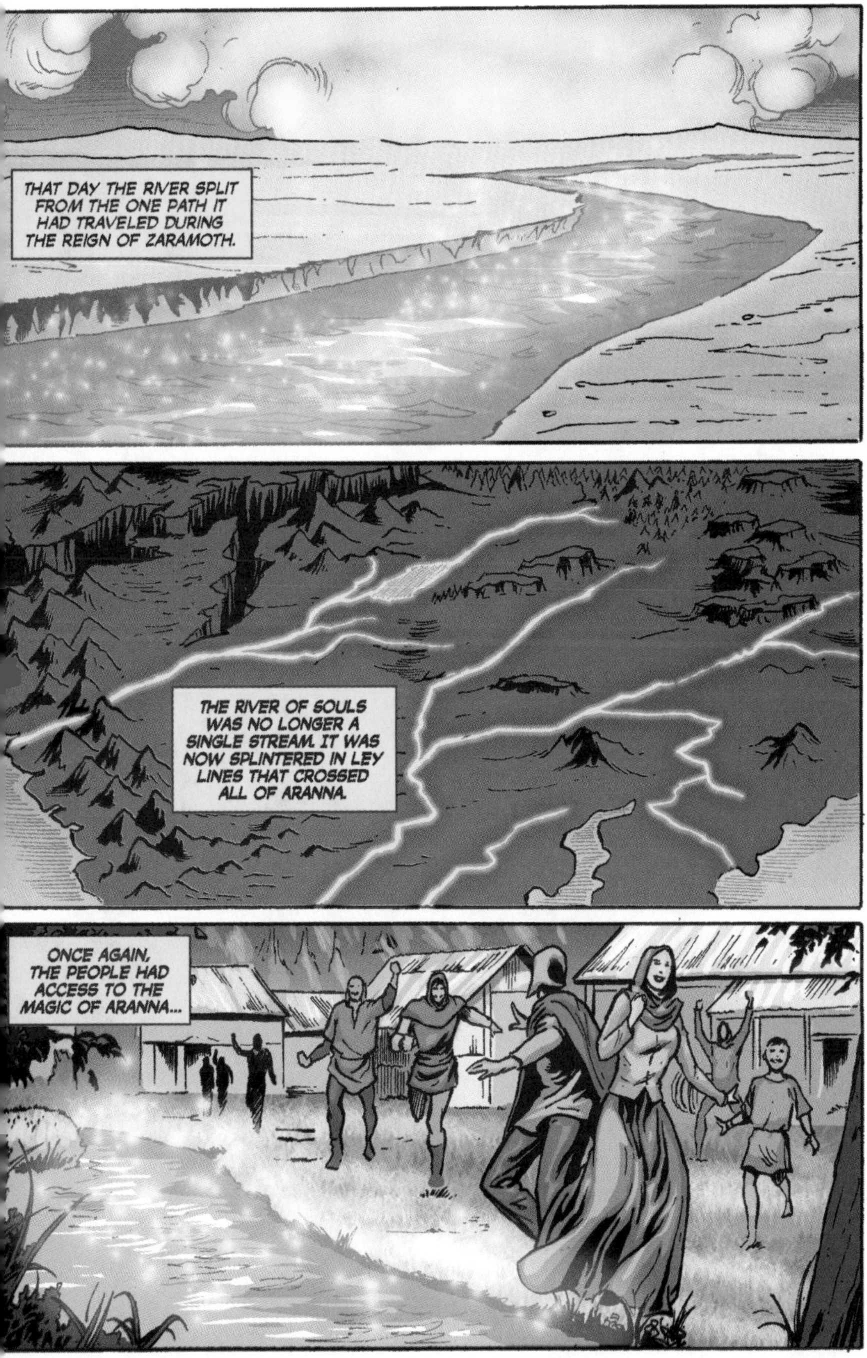
THAT DAY THE RIVER SPLIT FROM THE ONE PATH IT HAD TRAVELED DURING THE REIGN OF ZARAMOTH.
THE RIVER OF SOULS WAS NO LONGER A SINGLE STREAM. IT WAS NOW SPLINTERED IN LEY LINES THAT CROSSED ALL OF ARANNA.
ONCE AGAIN, THE PEOPLE HAD ACCESS TO THE MAGIC OF ARANNA...

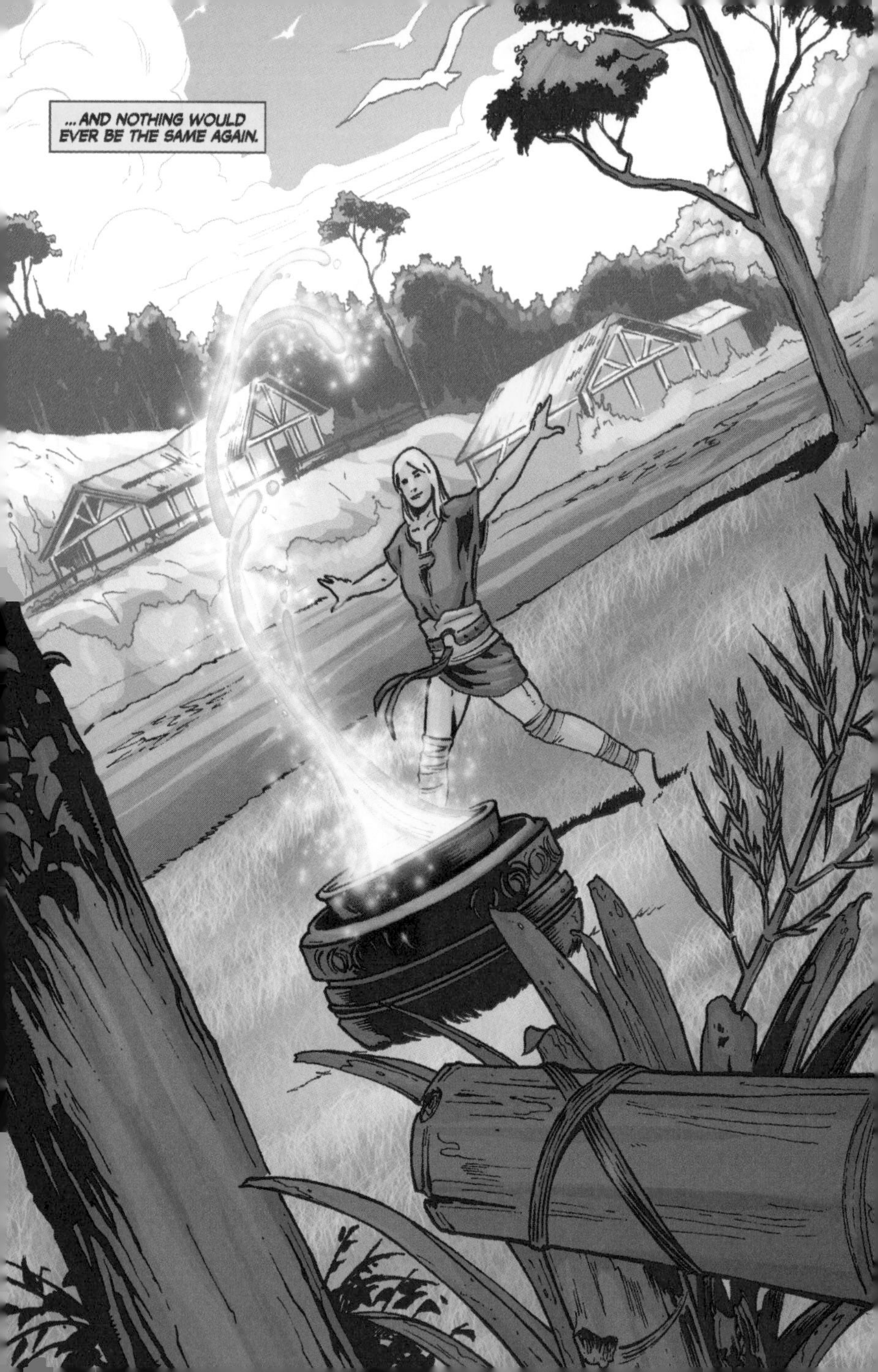
...AND NOTHING WOULD EVER BE THE SAME AGAIN.

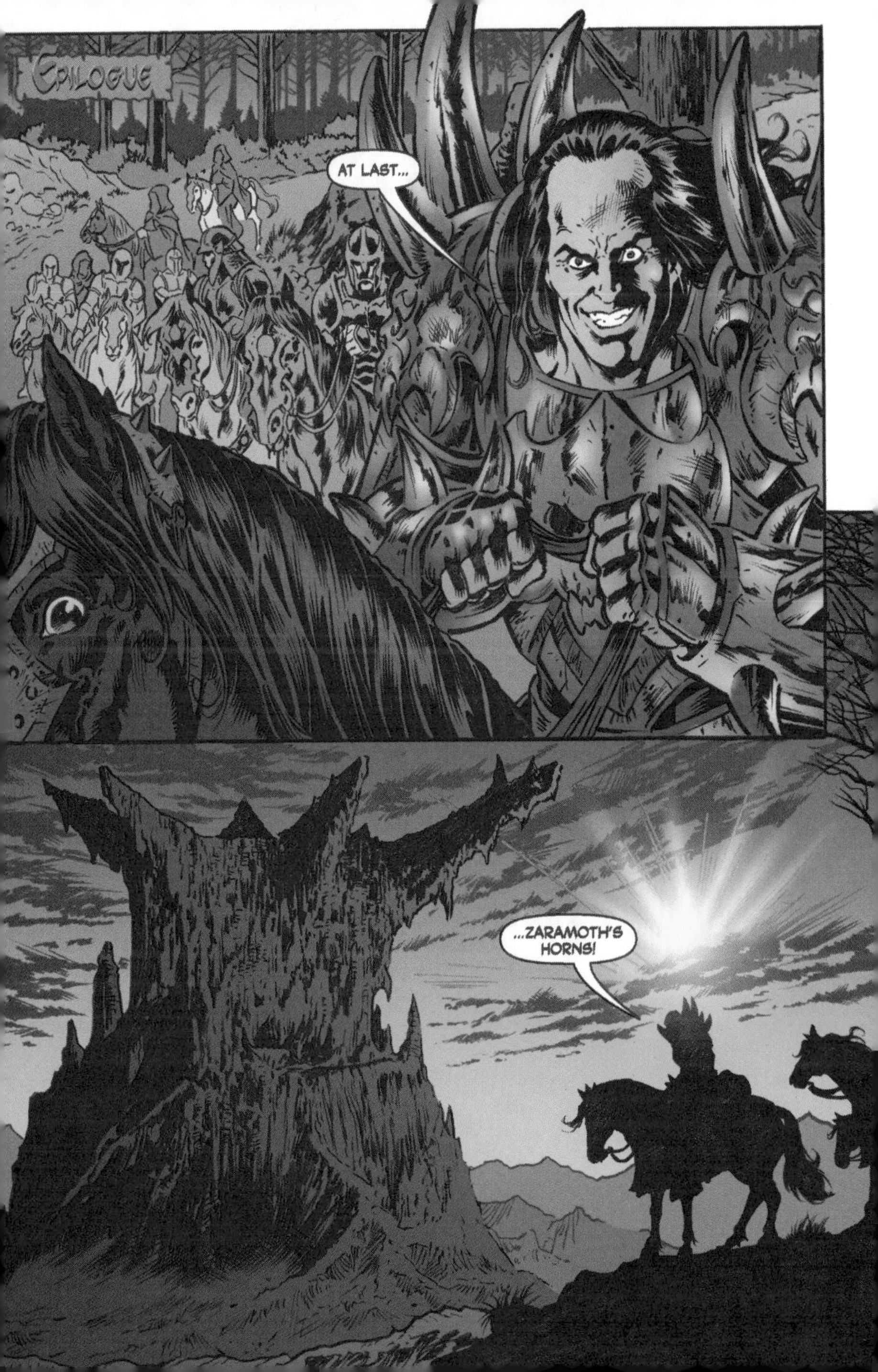
Epilogue
AT LAST...
...ZARAMOTH'S HORNS!

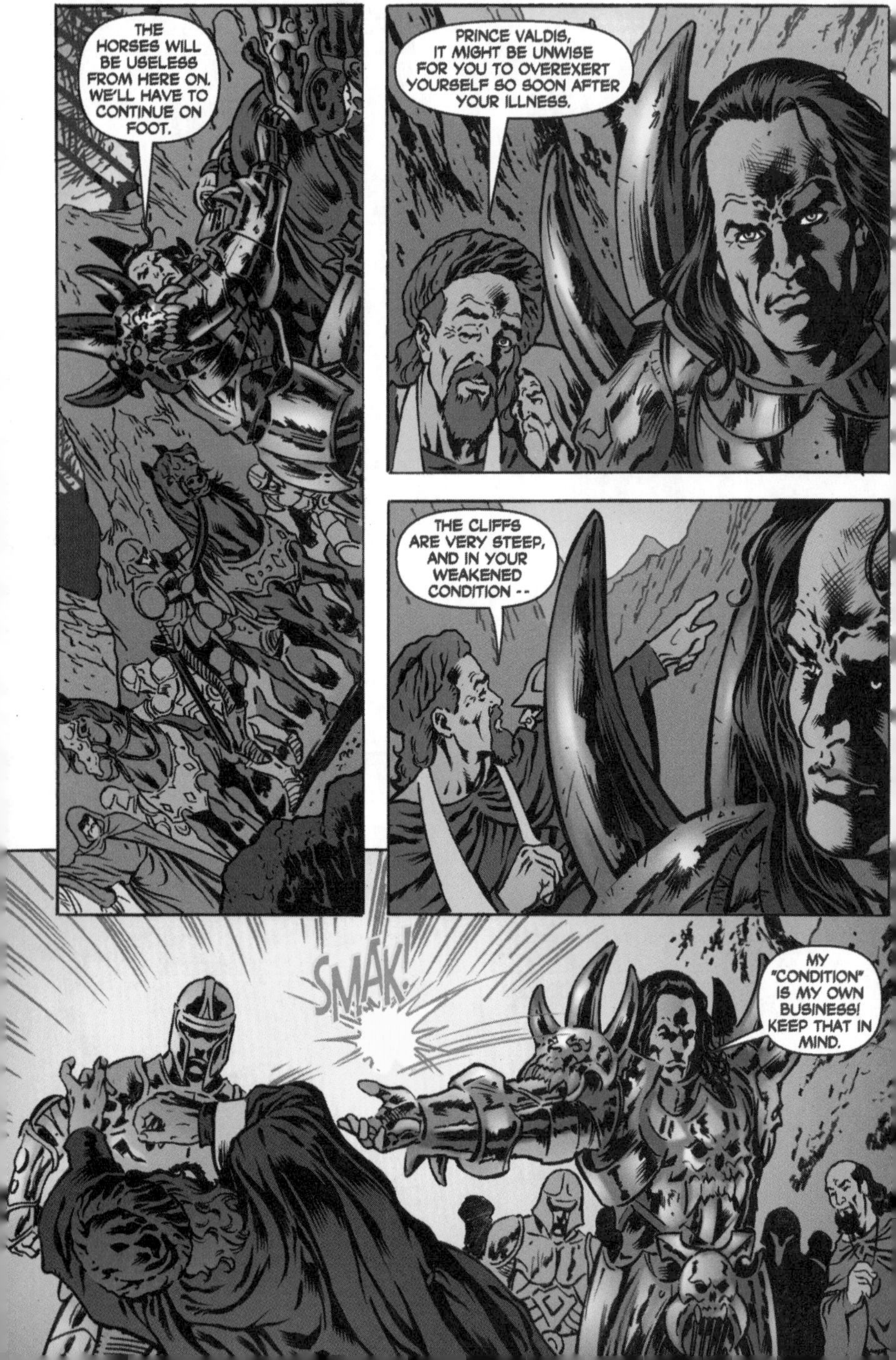
THE HORSES WILL BE USELESS FROM HERE ON. WE'LL HAVE TO CONTINUE ON FOOT.
PRINCE VALDIS, IT MIGHT BE UNWISE FOR YOU TO OVEREXERT YOURSELF SO SOON AFTER YOUR ILLNESS.
THE CLIFFS ARE VERY STEEP, AND IN YOUR WEAKENED CONDITION --
SMAK!
MY "CONDITION" IS MY OWN BUSINESS! KEEP THAT IN MIND.

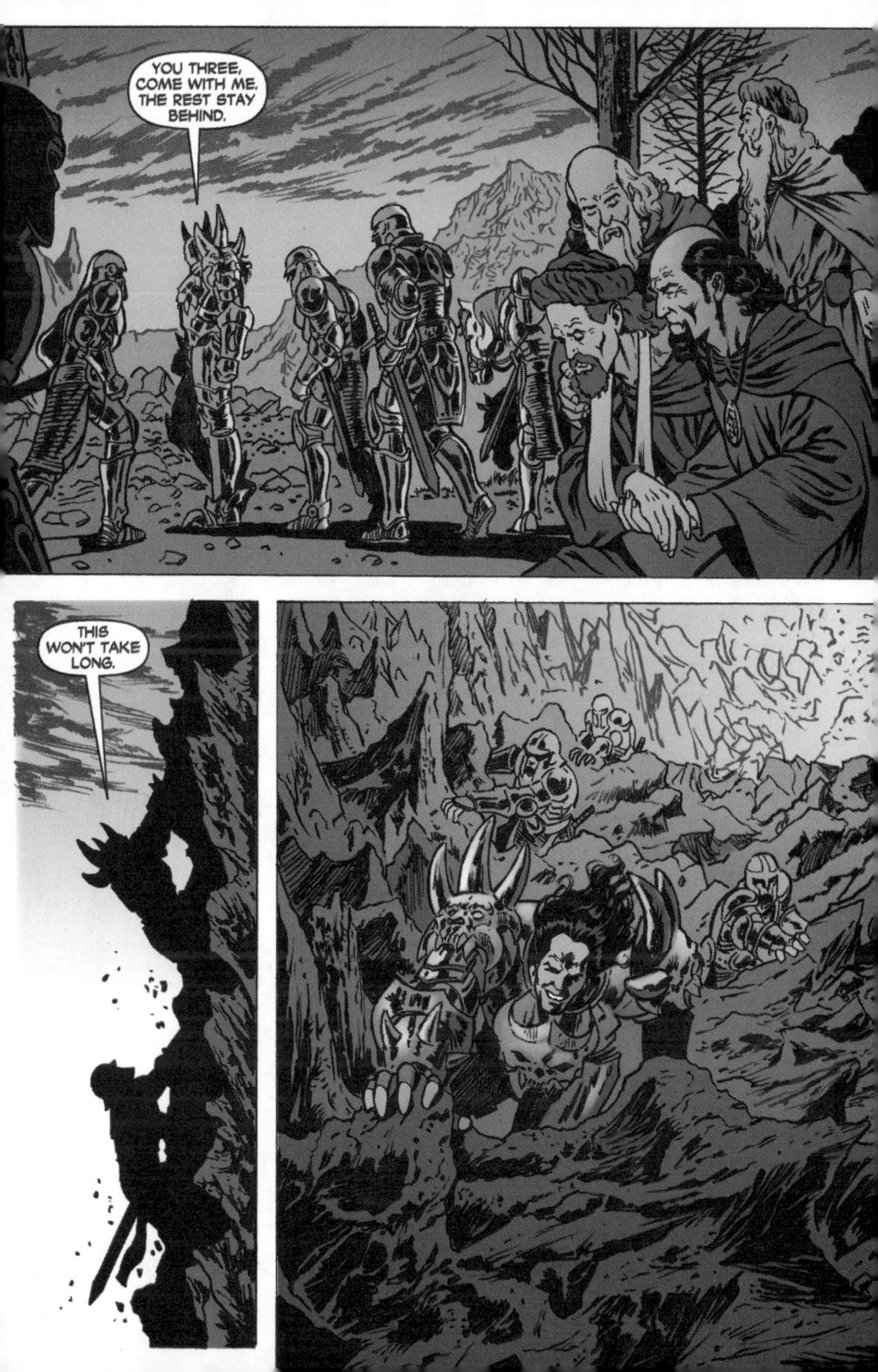
YOU THREE, COME WITH ME. THE REST STAY BEHIND.
THIS WON'T TAKE LONG.

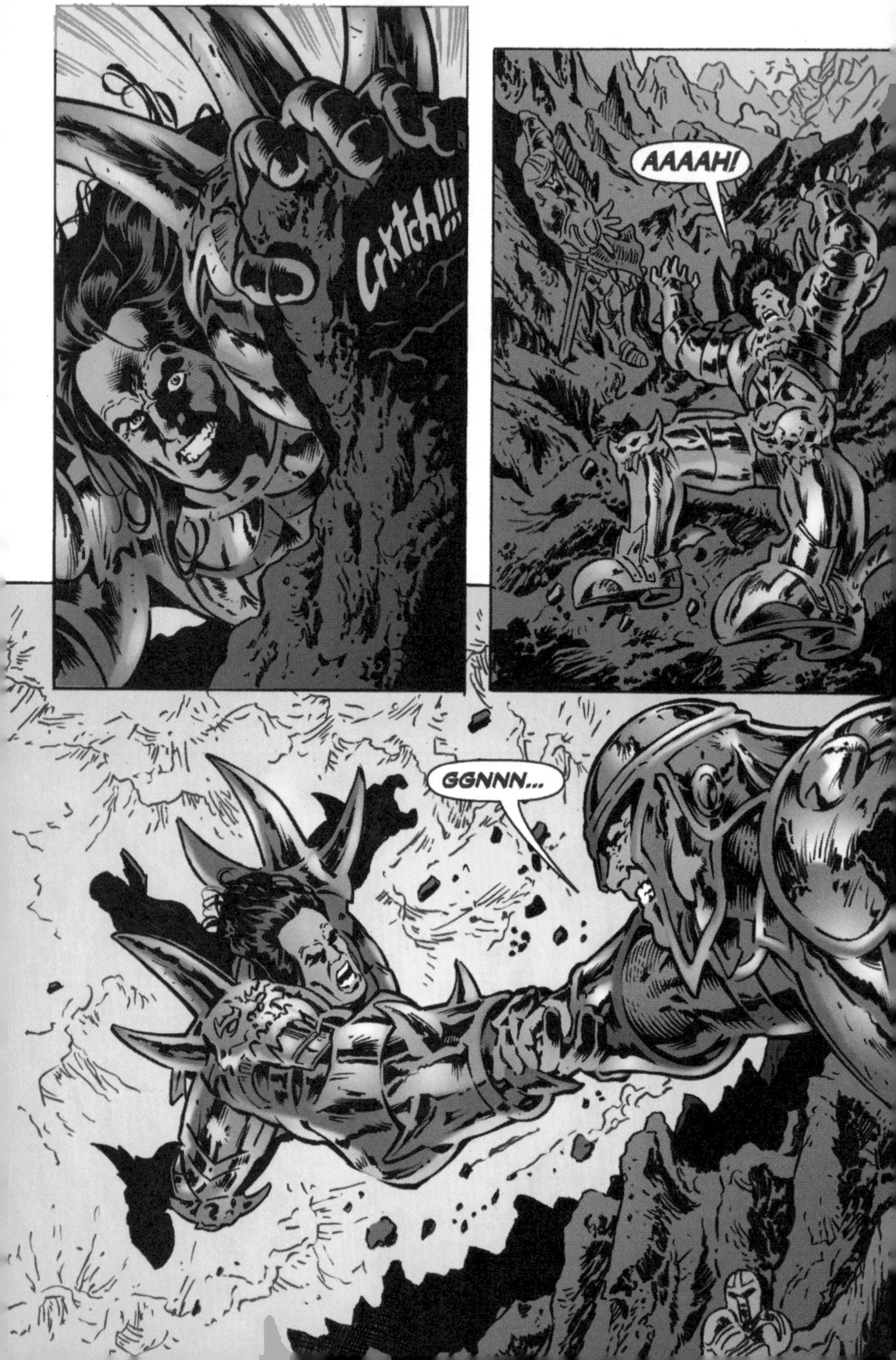
CRKTCH!!!
AAAAH!
GGNNN...

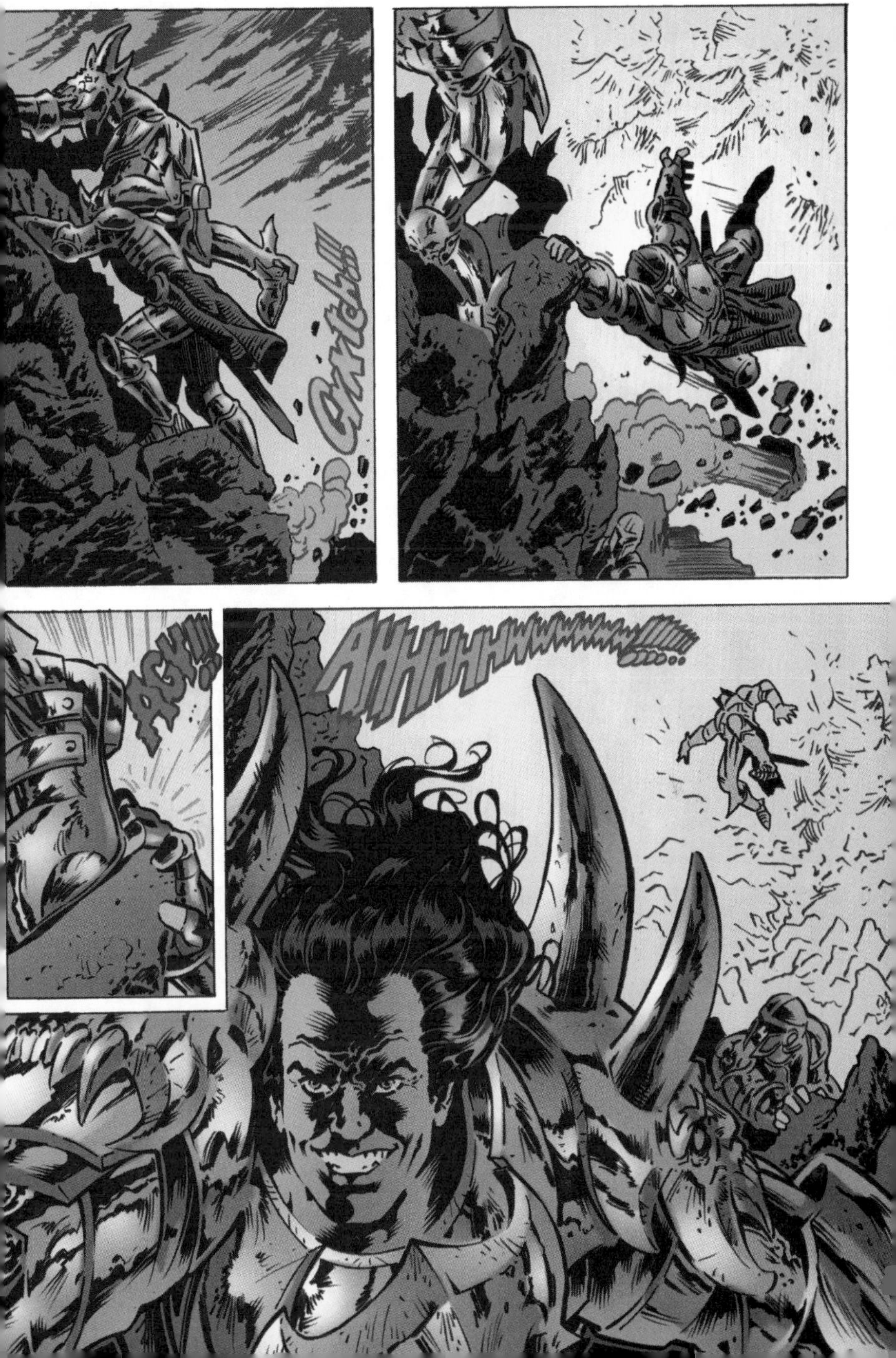
CRTCH!!!
AAGH!!!
AHHHHHWWWWW!!!ooo..

MMMMMBRR... ...RRRGGGG

ZSHKOW!

ZSHKOW!

YEEEAGH!

MMMBRRR

YES...

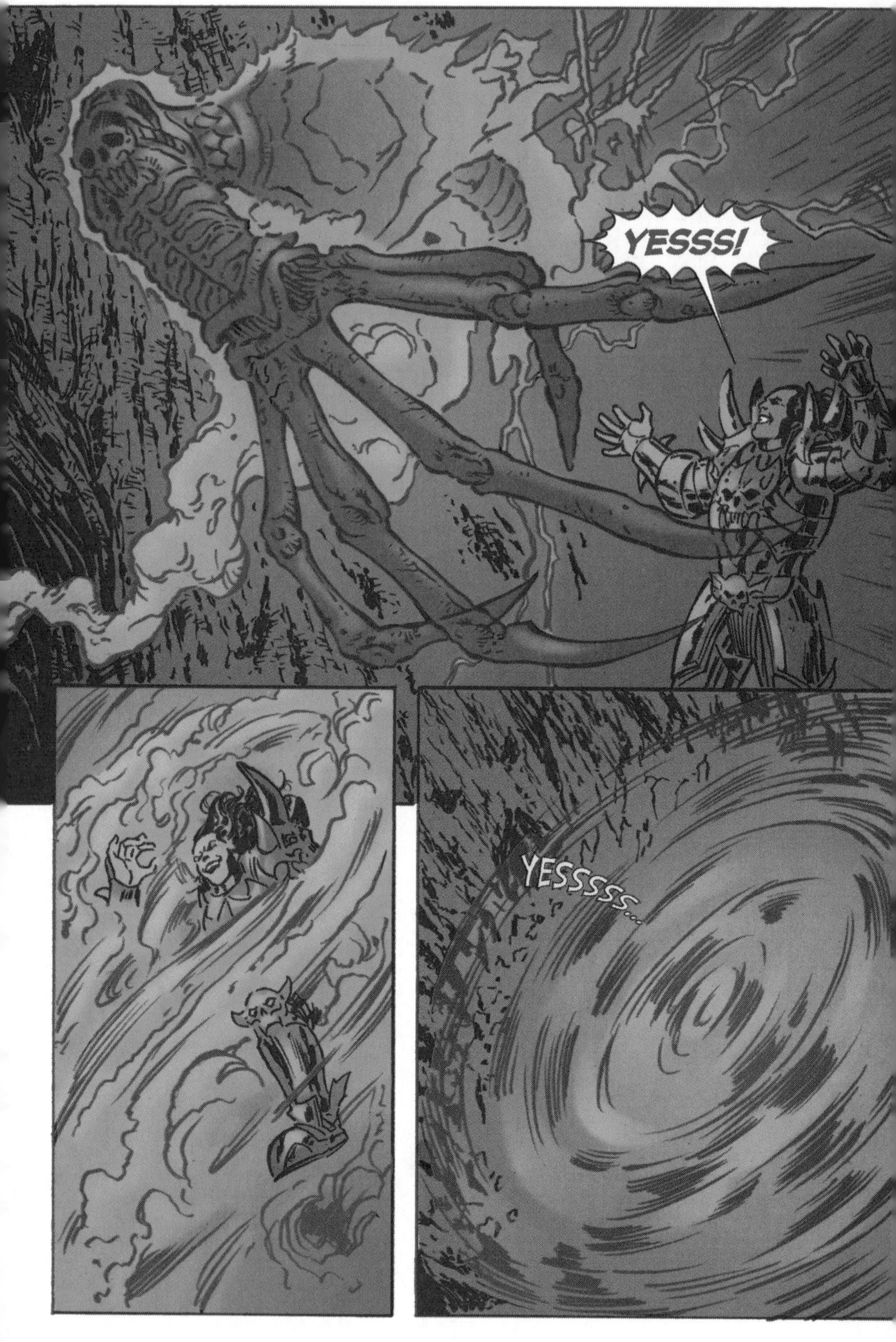
YESSS!
YESSSSS...

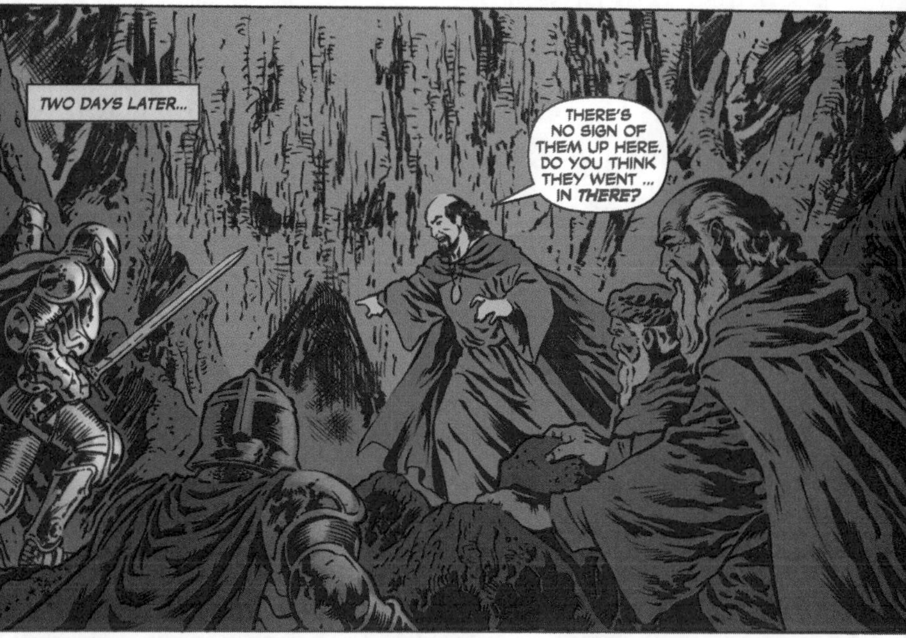
TWO DAYS LATER...
THERE'S NO SIGN OF THEM UP HERE. DO YOU THINK THEY WENT ... IN *THERE?*

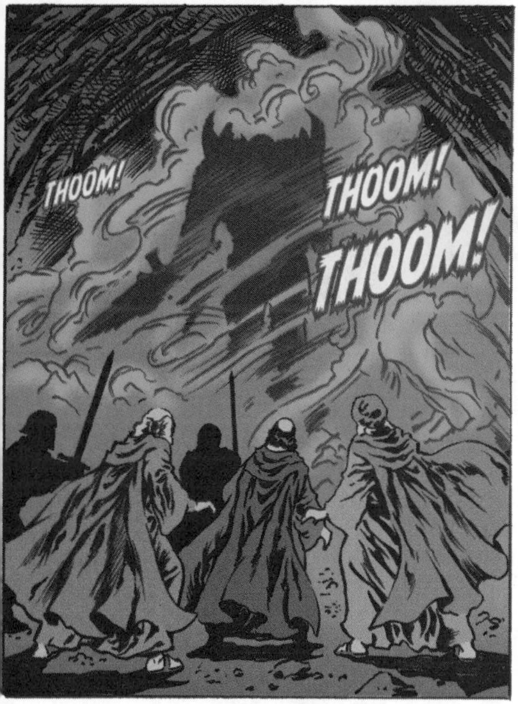
THOOM!
THOOM!
THOOM!

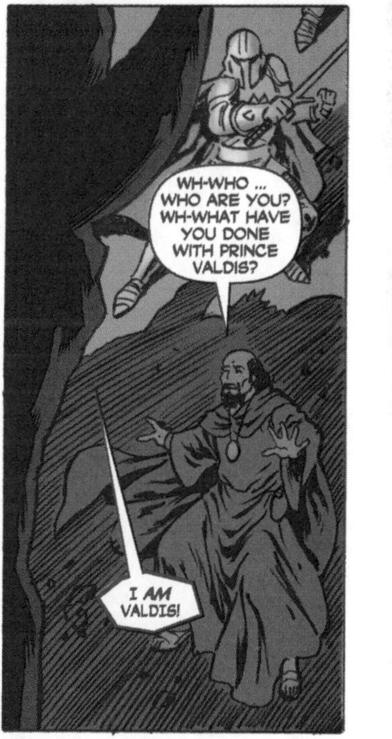
WH-WHO ... WHO ARE YOU? WH-WHAT HAVE YOU DONE WITH PRINCE VALDIS?
I *AM* VALDIS!

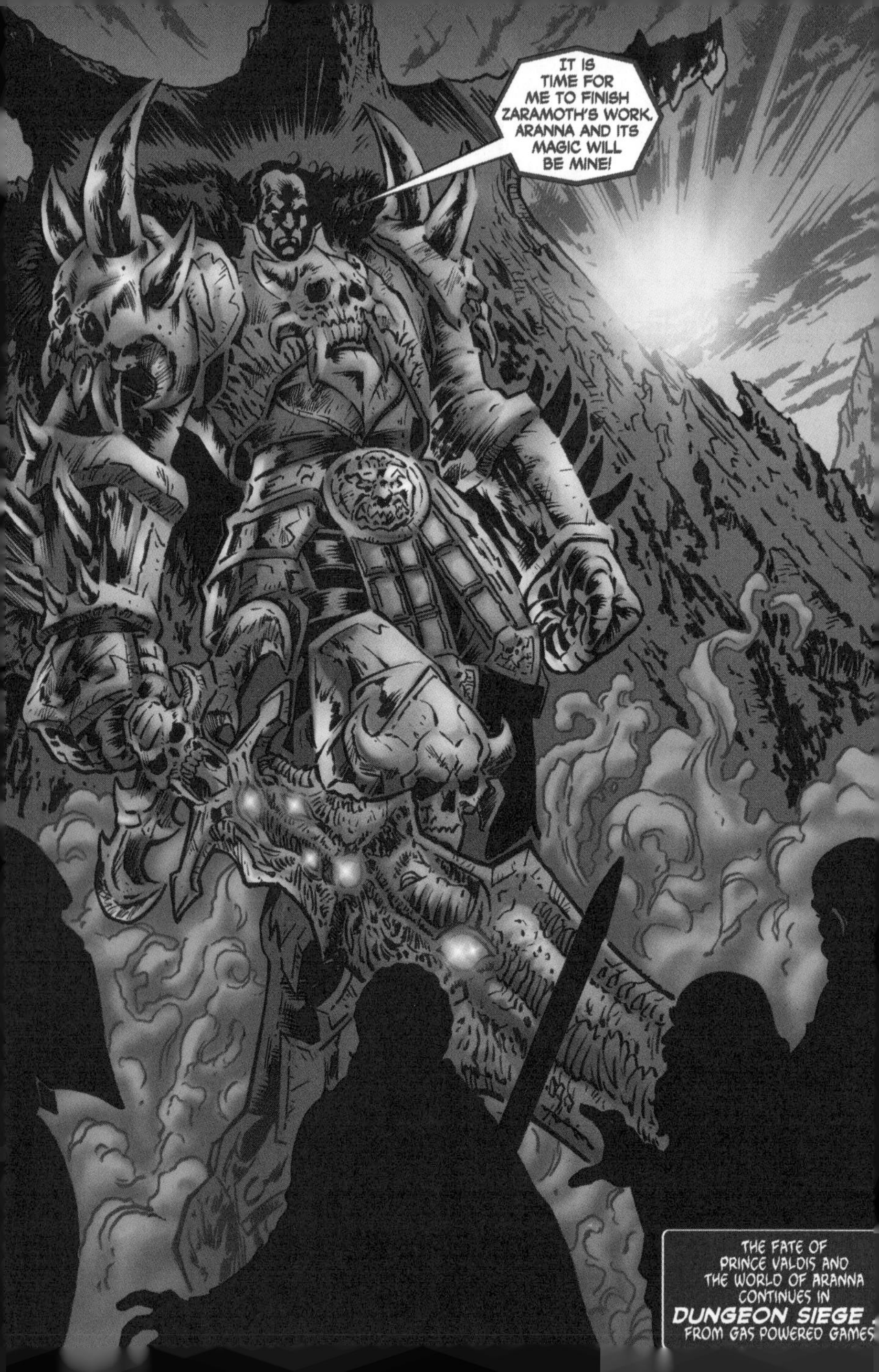
IT IS TIME FOR ME TO FINISH ZARAMOTH'S WORK. ARANNA AND ITS MAGIC WILL BE MINE!
THE FATE OF PRINCE VALDIS AND THE WORLD OF ARANNA CONTINUES IN DUNGEON SIEGE FROM GAS POWERED GAMES.

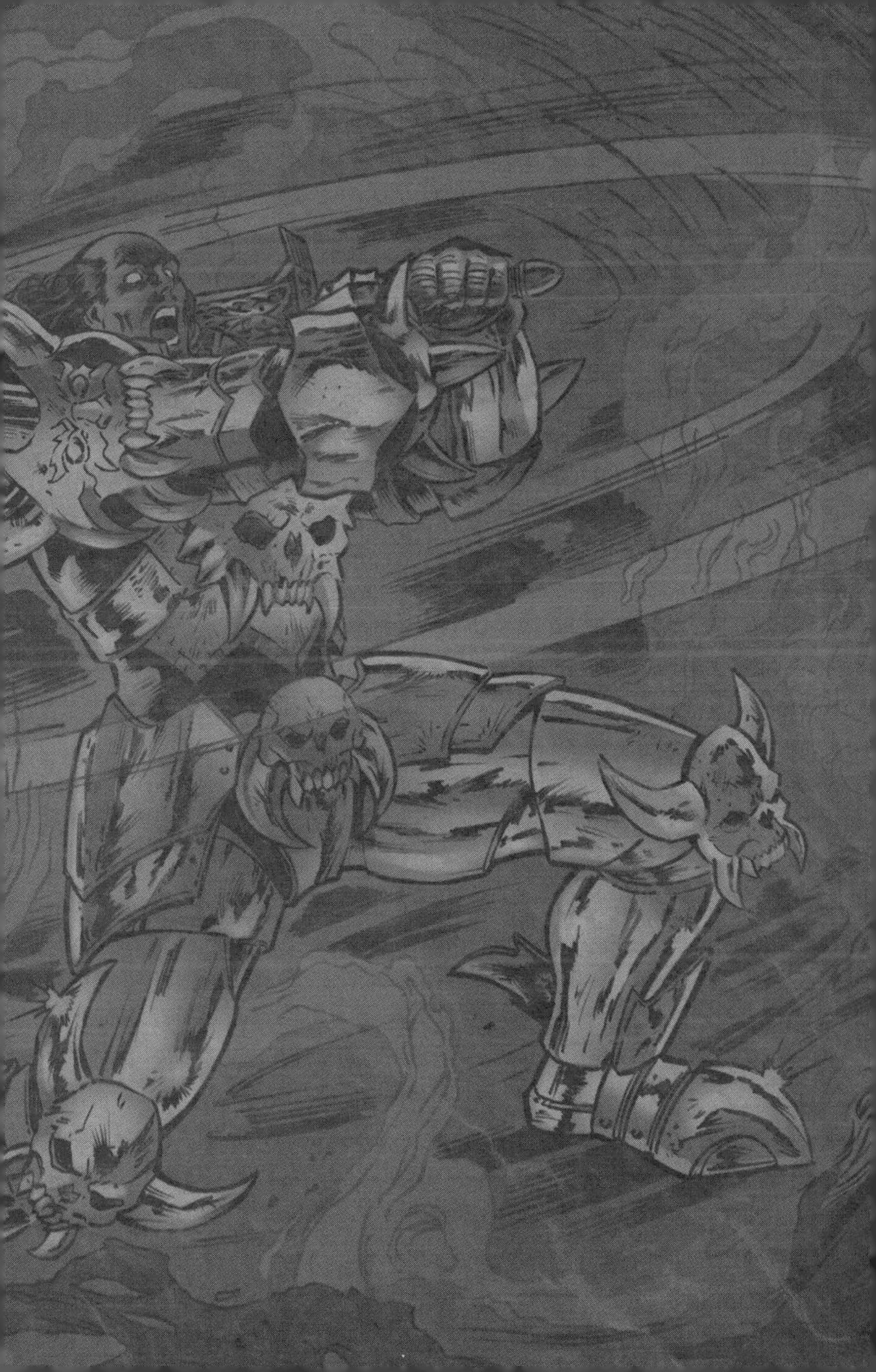